Secrets

of a

Mistress

How to Have an
Exciting
Love Affair With Your Man

Rose Smith

William Havens Publishing

Cover Design by Cindy Lombardo

William Havens Publishing
PO Box 81064
Albuquerque, NM 87198-1064 USA

WARNING:

Do NOT Read this book unless you want to become the only woman your man will ever desire!

Secrets of a Mistress will forever change the way you look at your intimate relationship.

First printing 1993

Library of Congress Number: 92-074746

Acknowledgements

My deepest thanks to the following people who helped make this book possible: Brenda Trujillo, Juanita Lott, Davidia Medley Burrell, Synthia Medley, Martha Gutierrez, Kay Griffin, Diane Christiano, Wanda Rodarte, Kim Forrester, Anna Gutierrez, Mary Jo Baca, Marjorie Lea, Patti Tatman, Dennis Hines, Monica Wolf, Elaine Beckett, Bridgett Alvarez, Karen Lujan, Anna Montoya, Kathy Morgan, Sherry Leeson, Janice Railey, Debi Randall, Marie Zehrung, Barbara Welsh, Jane Graham, Rochelle Maes, Veda Buckhanan, Diane Bennett, Geraldine Dunbar, Shirley Ragin, Winsom Thompson, Mamie Teague, Janice Thomas, Pat Edmonds, and Maria McDevitt. Special thanks to all the women who have taken the Married Mistress Seminar--this book is for all of you.

Special thanks to my children Bianca and James-Earl--I love you. And to my mom, Catherine Nixon, a very special lady who has *always* been in my corner. To my dad, William Nixon, who is no longer with us, thank you for all of your wisdom.

Dedication

To Earl Smith, my husband. One lifetime of loving and living with you is not enough. In our love affair with life, I'm glad we chose to live it together. I love you.

Names of individuals have been changed to protect their privacy.

Table of Contents

Part IV
Your Positive Mental Attitude

Part I
Affairs of the Heart

One

Putting Monogamy Back in Marriage

Announcement at the Teller Cage

I never thought it would happen to me, but I'll never forget that fateful day. I started my new teller job at a small bank, and this was to be my first day training behind the teller cage. Kathy, my trainer, held my attention until I noticed two women in my customer line. They were standing near the end of the line by the last silver pedestal with the draped burgundy divider. As the line moved them closer and closer to me, I could not help but notice their constant giggling and whispering. They were pointing in our direction.

I didn't know whether they were pointing at Kathy or me, but it was soon clear they were pointing at me. I wondered why they were laughing. I had never seen either one before. One was tall, short black hair, average build. She seemed to be initiating most of the giggling and whispering. The other woman was shorter with reddish brown hair. I still had no clue why they were laughing.

They finally made it to the front of the line. The tall woman placed her brown leather purse on the counter and looked directly at me while anxiously smacking on a piece of gum. "Can I help you?" I asked in a cheery voice, trying to ignore their obvious heckling mood. The tall woman spoke first. "Yeah," she spat out sarcastically. "I'm the one who's sleeping with your man! So what are you gonna do about it?" Her friend roared in uncontrollable, loud laughter as soon as she heard the announcement she anxiously witnessed. Kathy immediately stood up to leave, embarrassed by what she'd heard. "I don't want to get in your business," she said softly before leaving me to deal with the situation.

I don't even know if I saw Kathy leave or really even heard what she said. All I can remember is that woman's cruel announcement left me feeling like she smacked me in the stomach with a baseball bat; I felt like curling up in a defenseless ball. I couldn't say anything at first. My mouth felt so dry, like someone had stuffed cotton balls down my throat. I had no idea my husband was cheating on me. Her revelation knocked the wind out of me. After what seemed like an eternity, I finally spoke. With all the pride I could summon, I quietly said, "I hope what you just did to me never happens to you--I wouldn't wish it on anybody. I hope you never have to feel what I'm feeling right now." Both women stopped laughing, and they left. So did I. I left my job and my husband.

Though I'd left my ex-husband's infidelity hundreds of miles away, I carried the wrenching knot the other woman left in my stomach for years. Her announcement was the catalyst that ended my first marriage, but it was a marriage already on shaky ground. What this woman almost cost me is something much more precious.

That humiliating experience caused me to run from any intimate connection with a man for years. And when I met the man I later married, I was still running. I decided it was better to spend the rest of my days alone than be with an unfaithful man, and since my past experiences convinced me the majority of men were incapable of being faithful to one woman, I kept running.

After years of formidable patience and persistence, Smitty, the man I finally married convinced me to stop running. I get chills when I think of how I almost let that woman cost me the happy life I share with him and our two children, but Smitty's strong commitment to monogamy finally helped me look past my fears.

His vow to a one-on-one relationship faced a challenging test, however, when his military job sent him on a one year overseas assignment--*alone*. His vow to monogamy remained unwavered by our physical separation. This separation was also the beginning of our *marital affair* and was responsible for renewing our commitment to an intimate relationship filled with romance, passion, and excitement. Indulging in a marital affair with my husband changed our marriage forever and it did something else. It gave me an overwhelming sense of *power*. The knot the other woman had left in my stomach finally dissolved because I realized it is possible for a man and woman to choose to have an exciting monogamous relationship, and once a couple *truly* makes that commitment--*the other woman is powerless*.

For the first time, I realized it was up to my husband and me to infidelity-proof our relationship by not leaving it up to fate. We did this by making our relationship as exhilarating as any extramarital affair. It is with this in mind that I wrote the Married Mistress® Seminar, which this book is based on. This book teaches you how to have a passionate love affair with your man. If your husband or boyfriend is going to have an affair with anybody--he can have the most exciting and romantic affair of a lifetime--with *you*. The seminar and book are based not only on my personal experience but on interviews with therapists, happy couples, faithful and unfaithful men, wives, girlfriends, mistresses, and extensive research of medical journals, books, and magazine articles.

The Married Mistress

A married mistress is:

A woman who uses the power she possesses to keep her intimate relationship exciting, fulfilling, and monogamous.

As a married mistress, you'll discover the power you have to improve your relationship 100%! Women who have become married mistresses and the men who love them will share their stories about how satisfying and sensual their unions have become. The Married Mistress Seminar, along with its male counterpart, the Monogamous Male Seminar, teaches couples how to join the ranks of married or otherwise attached folks who are indulging in the same passionate ecstacy that *was* only experienced in extramarital affairs.

With the AIDS epidemic brutally slapping America in the face, many couples are choosing monogamy over fooling around. But fear of AIDS is not a substantial enough reason to turn to monogamy. People who are faithful because their partners are the only ones they desire are the ones who remain faithful. The utmost reason for a man and woman to devote themselves to one another is because *they want to--not because they have to.* Being *happily* monogamous is the key.

Infidelity's Irresistible Lure

It's a powerful aphrodisiac. 70% of married men and 40% to 50% of married women get swept into its sensual waters every year. It's electrifying, intense, and it offers an escape from day-to-day pressures. The extramarital affair can be very intoxicating--but it holds a huge downside. Many swept up by this forbidden liaison are all too aware of the guilt and pain associated with it.

What do you do? Tell someone looking for a more fulfilling relationship they should have thought about that before tying the knot? No--couples can gain the same intoxicating thrill and pleasure in their own torrid waters--*by indulging in a marital affair with their mates.* What's more, they can experience the euphoric high of an affair without any of the pain and remorse associated with it.

Studies conducted by Masters and Johnson show that "the overall pleasure of extramarital sex is somewhat lower for men and women in general than their overall sexual pleasure in their marriages." *Most people do not want to cheat.* Still, many people erroneously look to extramarital affairs to recapture lost passion. The marital affair offers couples a chance to recapture that passion--*together.*

How to Use This Book

This book is divided into four parts. The first part discusses the other woman, the extramarital affair, and the marital affair. To enjoy a true marital affair, it's important to understand the lure infidelity holds and uncover the mystique surrounding the other woman.

Part II discusses the importance of building your marital communication skills. You can't begin to reap the benefits of a marital affair if your intimate relationship isn't solid. Building the lines of communication is an integral part of any intimate relationship.

Part III involves the important role sex plays in your marital affair. In this section, you'll discover one of the most important elements of your marital affair, and you'll uncover the revealing secret of why the other woman seems so eager to make love all the time.

The final part talks about *you*. Your well-being, self-esteem, and positive mental attitude are inherent parts of your marital affair. Embarking on a marital affair has nothing to do with sacrificing your needs for your man. If you aren't content, your union will suffer. This section discusses ways for you to be as good to yourself as you are to everyone else around you.

Throughout this book, you'll find exercises for you to complete. These exercises help you determine what skills you need to utilize to strengthen your intimate relationship.

Use a separate notebook to record your answers so you'll have ample room for your thoughts. There is a *Married Mistress Workbook* available that includes each exercise in this book as well as a Love Notes diary for you to write down the many exciting escapades of your marital affair. You can order this book by sending $10.95 (plus $3.50 shipping) to:

> William Havens Publishing Company
> Married Mistress Workbook
> PO Box 81064 S-2
> Albuquerque, NM 87198-1064

Or call 505-260-0369 to order with VISA/Mastercard. (Make check or money order payable to William Havens Publishing Company.)

A Word to Single Women

Though the majority of research statistics on infidelity concentrate on married couples, this book is also for single or divorced women. Many single women have had experience with unfaithful boyfriends or live-in lovers. A single woman's pain is as real as a married woman's when she discovers her lover has been unfaithful.

Many divorced women have taken the Married Mistress Seminar. Women who have been in unpleasant relationships want to avoid repeating past mistakes or becoming attracted to another Mister Wrong. They also want to build better love skills *before* beginning new relationships. Katie, a woman in her late forties, took the seminar after being a divorcee for many years. After the seminar, she braved the singles scene by putting an ad in a magazine for singles, letting her prospects know she had taken the Married Mistress Seminar. The first man who responded to her ad was, to put it gently, not a good match for Katie. The second man she dated, however, turned out to be a perfect match. Seven months after she took the seminar, she and Tim got married.

So if you're single, divorced, widowed, or looking for Mr. Right, this book will help you put your future relationship or budding romance on the right track.

I'd Like You to Meet...

the real other woman. Researching infidelity and enjoying my marital affair with my husband gave me a better understanding of why affairs are irresistible to many. Enjoying a marital affair adds a spicy element to your relationship that many couples simply lose sight of. In my quest for knowledge, I also became more curious about the real other woman. Who is she? What does she do to captivate men? Can wives realistically compete with her? Can a marital affair be as fulfilling to a man or woman as an extramarital affair? I quickly realized there was only one person with the answers to all my questions--the other woman. With her help, this book answers the question:

• *What really goes on behind those hotel room doors?*

The answer may surprise you.

This book divulges everything you've ever wanted to know (but were too *angry* to ask) about the other woman and what really goes on in an extramarital affair. Who better to teach you how to have a tantalizing liaison with your man than the other woman? The only difference is you won't be hurting anyone; you'll only be helping yourself and your marriage.

Some of you probably feel you don't want to know anything about her. If you've experienced a sour relationship with the other woman, the last person you want to hear from is another one of her kind, right? Though she may anger you, I encourage you to listen because learning her secrets can teach you how to infidelity-proof your marriage. There is another reason to listen to her. Mistresses have been using information they have garnered from wives for years. Many of them use this information to ferret out good men. One mistress quoted in *Essence Magazine* had this to say about what she's learned by watching married men with their wives:

"They've lived with a woman through her many moods, and if they're good men--the only ones worth bothering with--they've also humored her, nursed her, on occasion fathered and mothered her, seen her weak and seen her strong. When you find a man who's lasted through all that, what a gem!"

What she and other mistresses fail to acknowledge is that this gem comes in a matching set! This book turns the tables on the other woman by teaching you how to keep your man out of her grasp. If 70% of married men cheat, that means upwards of 35 million wives will have to deal with the pain of infidelity, but it doesn't have to happen to you. And if it already has, you can prevent it from happening again.

The marital affair is not a cure-all for all infidelity-ills. There are numerous reasons men cheat and, as you will discover in Chapter Six, some of the reasons have absolutely nothing to do with their love partners. But, in cases where the intimate relationship has become too familiar a ground, or has suffered from an insufficient amount of passion, the marital affair can help re-ignite the flame.

For millions of wives and girlfriends, this book will unveil all the other woman's secrets so you can make your intimate bond stronger than ever--and forever out of her reach.

To begin your journey to passionate monogamy, turn the page to meet the woman whose secrets will teach you everything you need to know.

Two

Who Is She?

Sexy Seductress

"I'm your worst nightmare. I'm young, blonde, beautiful, and I'm after your husband. I can get him, too. Most men find me irresistible. They regress to a child-like state when I enter their lives because I render them helpless under my spell. Oh, I know they can never explain how they become involved with me. They usually make excuses and mumble those tired words--*it just happened.* Let me tell you, it never just happens--I *make* it happen:

"A sudden hush overcomes the crowded apartment as I seductively enter. When I walk to the other side of the room to greet the hostess, I take every pair of eyes with me. Men tell me I have a great body; I work out faithfully. My thighs have never suffered the negative results of one fudge brownie--I don't do sweets. I laughed once when one of my lovers told me that my long, silky legs stretch all the way into tomorrow. My favorite dress when I'm on the prowl is my short, black number--the tantalizing one with the low-cut front. It fits my voluptuous body like a second skin; it's especially snug around my buns of steel. Mid-thirties--no, not my age--my hips and bust size. My waist and age? Low twenties.

"On my way over to the hostess I spot my first victim--he's the one with the drool dripping down his chin. His wife freezes up as I cozily brush up against him when I walk by. I lock my aqua blues onto his, instantly putting him in a hypnotic trance. I laugh to myself as he sheepishly but delightfully grins like a child about to devour a delicious chocolate fudge sundae. He's lost in my bewitching spell.

"Oh, excuse me," I seductively purr, "I didn't mean to spill your drink."

"I-I-It's O.K., he nervously sputters, "I-I think I did it all by myself." He tries to gather his composure while wiping the wetness off his chin with his cocktail napkin--then he anxiously asks me a question. His voice is low and husky--barely audible. "Speaking of drinks, can I get you one?"

"Not now honey," I drawl sweetly while hypnotically gazing in his eyes, "but do save me one for later."

"I'll be right here," he dizzily consents as if he's just become my humbled servant.

"Yes, Harold, *we'll* be right here," his wife forcefully interjects while swiftly moving closer, taking her 'place' by his side.

"At first he looks at her like he forgot who she was. Then he looks embarrassed. The harsh, judgmental look on her face reminds him of his childhood neighbor. He remembers how angry his neighbor was when she caught him red-handed playing 'doctor' with her daughter. He was only eight at the time.

"That's when I take a moment to glance his wife's way. With one look my icy blue eyes tell her that I can have her man anytime I want him.   She looks helpless--she knows he's trapped in my titillating web of lust. I've won, and she's lost. I enticingly throw my head back while shaking my honey-golden mane of hair away from my face. Then I seductively make my way over to flirt with my next easy mark--someone else's man.

"I know you wish you could shoot darts out of your eyes and aim them right for my delicate peaches and cream complexion about now. You probably want to pull my hair out and rip my face off. You want to make me stop sleeping with married men. I know I'm every wife's worst enemy.

"I'm the other woman: seductress, mistress, home-wrecker. I can come into your life and abruptly tear apart what you've spent 5, 10, even 25 years to build. And I can do it *so easily*. Sometimes, all it takes is an inviting flutter of my long, dark eyelashes. This year 50% to 70% of married men will have an extramarital affair with *me;* your worst nightmare. And I can guarantee the numbers would be even higher if they included live-in lovers and boyfriends in those statistics.

The *Real* Other Woman

"When I do steal your husband, chances are you won't even know it *because you won't be looking for me.* You'll be looking for the woman I just described. The seductive blonde with the voluptuous legs and skin-tight dress. You probably won't even see me coming because I don't look anything like her. More often than not, she is the stuff of mythical mistresses.

"That usually works to my advantage. Because when you're looking for the luscious blonde, you'll miss me. My hair can be mousy brown, jet black, or even dishwater blonde, curly or bone straight. My eyes can be sea green, baby blue, or deep chocolate brown. I can weigh anywhere from 110 to 220 pounds. I come in all shapes, sizes, and colors, and I can be young, middle-age, or mature. I can be a teacher, waitress, secretary, or lonely housewife. Your best friend, next-door neighbor, or even a relative. I'm a woman--*just like you, no different*.

"Why then if I'm like any average woman, does a married man risk all to have a fling with me? Because it's not about what I look like or who I am--*it's all about how I make a man feel*. Though you may not like what I represent, I can reveal to you what men really look for in an extramarital affair. Believe me, it isn't anything that you can't do in your marriage.

An Insider

"I don't bewitch husbands, and I don't cast love spells, so don't give me full credit for wrecking happy homes. I usually have an accomplice in my lustful crime of passion. This person helps me tremendously because she's an insider who does a good job of botching up her own marriage. All that leaves for me is coming in and taking over where she leaves off.

"Where does my accomplice leave off? Depends. She usually helps me by doing a number of things like: ignoring her mate, forgetting why she married in the first place, putting her career over her marriage, having a perpetual 'headache' for months on end, or always putting the children first, leaving the marriage to take care of itself. In other words: *My accomplice leaves the door wide open for me to come in and steal her man.*

"Yes, many times my insider is *the wife*. Most married men do not really want to entangle themselves in an extramarital affair. Few people enjoy sneaking around because of all the unhealthy repercussions it can cause. A small percentage of men are unfaithful just because they can get away with it. However, the majority tell me they cheat because they are lonely or unfulfilled in their marriages. Sure, a husband needs to tell his wife if he feels she is not meeting his needs. But sometimes his spouse won't listen, and many times he'll just take the easy route and get what he needs from me. I can't worry about why your man cheats, that's your problem, not mine.

"I know you wives love to blame me when your men cheat on you, but what about them? What about you? Sleeping with a married man is wrong, but it takes three people to make a triangle. As a wife or girlfriend, you need to take a long, hard look at your intimate relationship, your man, and the part you play in this threesome.

"Not all married women help me. There is one kind of wife I can't stand because she makes my task difficult. Her man is the one in the crowd my charms have no influence on. He's impenetrable. I don't even waste my time on him because he's too happy at home to think about me--he's too busy thinking about her. She's his best friend, his mistress, his partner, and his bond with her is rock solid.

"This type of woman irritates me. When I'm after my prey, her man is the one I avoid because I don't want to waste my efforts on him. When I do flirt with him, he politely flashes his wedding ring telling me he's flattered but happily taken. That's my cue to go elsewhere. So I just make sure I concentrate on the men whose women make it easy for me. I can spot them a mile away.

"The annoying truth is, *I envy you.* You can make your intimate bond as strong as you want it to be. I can't come into your home and take over your role as loving partner and super mom. But you can fill my shoes any day. You can experience the same excitement I do when I'm having an affair by having a *marital affair* with your man. When your man lusts after me, he doesn't really see me--he sees *you.* More than likely, he's using me to awaken the erotic passion he once shared with you. But I don't care if I start out as your replacement because I know he'll eventually realize I'm the person who's giving him the love he needs. My goal is to replace you by being the one to re-ignite the flame that once sizzled between you two--if *you* don't do it first."

Three

The Witch Hunt Begins

"That Witch!"

Hearing egotistical words from any mistress used to make me tense with impetuous anger. As a happily married woman, I do not like to hear any of them brag about destroying marriages. My first instinct is to tune them out and refuse to let what they say get to me; however, I saw something on the Geraldo Rivera Show one day that forever changed the way I view mistresses.

I was half-heartedly listening to Geraldo while dusting my furniture, when he abruptly captured my attention by giving the address of a mistress club. I stood there watching the rest of the show while holding my furniture polish in one hand and letting the dust-rag dangle in the other. Apparently, a woman organized this club to help mistresses deal with the pain of loving someone else's husband! I continued watching in shock and disbelief that such an organization even existed.

The representative of the club looked like she could be president of the local PTA. She had mousy brown hair, no makeup, and weighed about 180 pounds. And though I didn't catch her name, I never forgot her message. This woman actually encouraged the audience to empathize with the mistresses sharing their stories of anguish. She talked about the pain a mistress suffers when she loves a married man. The hours wasted waiting for him to slip away, the nights she spends anxiously waiting for his call, all the holidays she spends alone wishing she was the wife. Unfortunately, sometimes she does get her wish.

Then she said something that remains engraved in my brain. She revealed that she receives letters *daily* from mistresses around the country who are experiencing this often self-induced pain. At the time, I had no idea they were out there in such large numbers, but they are. *The Hite Report On Male Sexuality* acknowledges that 72% of the men surveyed who have been married for more than two years have committed adultery. I had to ask, what is the other woman doing to cause this, and how can wives stop her? It occurred to me while watching Geraldo that it isn't the mistress who needs encouragement for creating love triangles, it is *the wife* who needs support in keeping her marriage from suffering at the hands of another woman.

Most of the women in the audience were about as sympathetic to the mistresses on the television panel as I was. "How can you be so cruel?" "How could you sleep with your sister's husband?" "What possessed you to steal your daughter's boyfriend?" "She was your best friend!" "Don't you have a heart!?" Comments like these poured out of the crowd. Evidence of disapproval swept through the audience, yet the obvious disdain did not keep the mistresses from flaunting their adultery. On top of that, they wanted sympathy to boot!

A Classic Mistake Many Wives Make

If you share the same view of the other woman I did, hearing anything she has to say about stealing someone else's husband usually brings about a separation process in your mind. You tell yourself she's not anything like you. You aren't capable of stealing another woman's husband and then trying to justify your behavior. She is abnormal, different, a witch in disguise. Yet, that same separation process may allow you to believe she is different in other ways:

> ♦ She's alluring, mysterious,
> ♦ She's prettier, sexier,
> ♦ I can't compete with her,
> ♦ She can give him what he needs; I can't.

That's where wives and girlfriends make their first major mistake. The other woman is no different from you or me. Her moral values may be different, nevertheless, she does share a common bond-- she is a woman. *She is no prettier, no sexier, no better than most wives.*

The next mistake is the way wives react to her. Heated anger, fierce fury, and complete frustration send their emotions into override.

Shockwaves race through them when they see her coming. They often lose the ability to remain rational. And she can have another devastating affect. She can scare some wives and cause them to doubt their feminine lures.

The thought that she has some kind of charisma they don't briefly plays on their minds. It's at that moment most married women tune her out. They quickly tell themselves she's not worth the effort--she doesn't have anything they want. But she does--she has power. She can rip through an intimate bond like an angry tornado, destroying everything in her path--the spouse, the children, and the happy home. Adultery is an extremely difficult pill for any marriage to swallow. Only 50 percent of marital unions survive after infidelity.

However, as the wife or girlfriend, you have precisely the same power, only instead of using your power to destroy, you use it to make your intimate relationship stronger than ever. You have the power to become the mistress in your intimate relationship--and together, you and your mate have the power to infidelity-proof your relationship.

But what if your mate has already strayed? What if the other woman has already pounced upon your marriage and tried to break-up your happy home--is there hope? *Yes, there is.* The next chapter talks about dealing with the pain of infidelity and keeping it from happening again.

Four

Powers of a Mistress

"Inside my head I am screaming, screaming, screaming. Dear God let me die; let this plane crash this second, give me oblivion. Please! Please! I can't stand the pain, I can't live, I want to die, now, this minute." Jo Fleming (a pen name for a well-known celebrity wife) wrote those words in her book, *His Affair*, which takes readers through her wrenching ordeal with her famous husband's infidelity. Finding out your lover has been unfaithful is like being in a head-on collision. Usually, with little or no warning, his affair invades your lane, and your world crashes around you. The results are often debilitating for your intimate relationship and your weakened self-esteem.

Sally, one of my clients, is eye-arresting. She is a thirty-eight-year-old classic beauty with porcelain-smooth skin and copper-red spiral curls that strikingly compliment her sky blue eyes. It is hard to imagine this slender beauty feeling insecure about anything, but she recently found out she has reason to feel threatened. Her husband of seven years left her after admitting he's been sleeping with another woman. Seated in my office, Sally squeezes her monogrammed handkerchief between her delicate hands and chokes back her tears as she expresses her sense of helplessness.

"He left me. I think I want him back, but I don't know if I can live with the fact that he's slept with someone else. Anyway, it really doesn't matter because even if I wanted him back, I can't do anything about it. I know we need to work on our marriage, but now he won't even give me the chance. Things were great between us when we first got married. Rob told me he never wanted anyone the way he wanted me. I knew we were drifting apart, we both were so busy with our careers, but I figured the situation would work itself out. I noticed how distant he's been lately--then he hit me with this. I feel so lost.

I don't know what I'm going to do. How could he want to throw away a seven-year-investment in our marriage on her?"

When Sally and Rob were the only parties involved in their intimate union, they shared control. But when Rob's extramarital affair intruded upon their marriage, his mistress successfully stripped Sally of much of her power. Now, whatever happens between Rob and Sally is contingent upon what happens between Rob and the other woman in their lives.

Besides being a woman who sleeps with a married man, Webster also defines a mistress as: *A woman who rules others or has control, authority, or power over something.* You are the mistress in your marriage. What you have control over is your intimate union. The key is making sure you don't ever share your power with another woman.

Dealing With the Affair

No wife ever wants her happy twosome to become a painful threesome. Like Sally, some of you who have attended the Married Mistress Seminar or who read this book have already experienced the excruciating turmoil of finding out your mate has strayed. You know firsthand about the other woman's destructive ability to turn your life upside down. If you've ever dealt with an unfaithful lover, one thing you do know is that you never want to encounter infidelity again--it's too painful.

Infidelity ripped apart Carol's marriage of twenty-five years. "It was as if someone tore my insides out," she remembers. "We raised two sons together. He met her at work; they were both attorneys. I found out later that when she saw him in court, she asked the judge to introduce him to her. The judge told her my husband was married, but she went after him anyway. When they tied the knot, guess who did the honors? The judge who introduced them is the one who married them."

Diane had just had her third child when she discovered her husband of thirteen years had been dating another woman for over a year. "I didn't know I *had* that many tears--I cried buckets. He never went anywhere for years, and all of the sudden, he started staying out all night, then he started dating a younger woman. I've tried everything to get him back. I have three kids, and I don't know what to do. I just feel so helpless."

Helpless

That feeling is a common thread among women who confront infidelity head-on. Many who believe that they would immediately leave an unfaithful man find it's not so easy to turn around and walk out the door.

"I don't know what to do next," confessed Susan who thought she would leave without delay when she found out her husband had been sleeping around. "It's not easy to leave someone you love, and I have the kids to consider."

We aren't equipped with a convenient on/off switch for love. One solution to avoiding this feeling of helplessness is to keep your relationship from the threatening lure of adultery. But even if you have survived infidelity, you can keep it from happening again. You can still build a strong foundation in your marriage. To do that, you need to understand the enticement the other woman offers.

What Does He See in Her, Anyway?

In surveying over thirty men who have had affairs lasting at least two years, I asked them what they saw in the other woman. Though this is not a scientific study, it does show the following similarities in their answers:

- ♦ She builds up my ego and makes me feel good about myself,
- ♦ I feel good when I'm around her,
- ♦ She offers me an escape from the pressures of everyday life,
- ♦ She doesn't constantly put me down,
- ♦ We understand and respect each other,
- ♦ She excites me and makes sex fun,
- ♦ She takes good care of herself,
- ♦ She's independent.

Is there anything on that list that you cannot do? Any woman can. *There is absolutely nothing the other woman does for her lover that you cannot do better.* And the more you know about the lure infidelity offers, the better equipped you'll be in keeping it from interfering with your intimate relationship. The first step for many wives already facing this hurtful situation is acknowledging it.

The Last to Know

Why is the wife always the last one to know? Many wives find themselves asking that very question when they uncover their husband's extramarital affair. "The signs were there," remembers one wife. "I just chose to ignore them." Her comments illustrate my next point well. Many times the wife discovers the infidelity last because she really doesn't want to know her husband is cheating on her.

Renee found out about her husband's extramarital escapades long after the fact, but it wasn't because the signs weren't there; he stayed out all night on their honeymoon. After years of turmoil with this man, she finally left him. She admits now that his staying out all night was a sign that her new marriage was in serious trouble but says she wasn't ready to face up to that until many similar episodes later. "I just didn't want to acknowledge I had made a bad choice."

A dear friend of mine died of cancer a few years ago. Even when Alice felt the first tiny lump in her breast, she refused to go to the doctor for help. Had she acknowledged the lump and sought medical help early, she may have saved her life. But acknowledging the lump meant confronting cancer, and that meant facing a terrifying death. By turning a blind-eye to her lump, she was in denial. She stayed in denial until the cancer eventually robbed her of her life.

Facing infidelity is difficult and agonizing. Like cancer, sometimes it's terminal. It can kill your marriage. But if you do suspect your man is cheating and you turn the other way, or you avoid the signs, like Alice's cancer, his extramarital affair will usually catch up with you in the end.

Accomplice to the Crime

By being the last to know, women help their lovers cheat on them everyday. There are also other ways women help men stray. If you:

- ♦ Turn your head the other way,
- ♦ Forgive him time and time again or,
- ♦ Excuse him for just being a man,

you help him commit adultery.

--*Turning the Other Way*--

Knowing that your husband is cheating and choosing not to acknowledge it is like putting a bomb in a pressure cooker. When the lid blows off, it will explode in your face. By confronting his affair, at least the two of you can deal with it openly and move on from there. When Renee finally addressed her first husband's infidelity, she dealt with it and moved on. After severing all ties with her former husband, she found a man who was worthy of all the love she had to give. They have been happily married for over five years, and she says having a monogamous man is one of the most secure feelings a woman can have.

--*Chronic Forgiveness*--

Experts confirm that a woman is usually quicker to forgive her husband's unfaithfulness than if the situation reversed itself. Many men simply will not stick around after their wives have cheated on them. Our society frowns on women who have affairs, and men do not expect women to be unfaithful. However, society conditions women to expect men to cheat.

Don't misunderstand me. I'm not suggesting the minute any woman finds out her beau has strayed--he's out. It's never that simple, and every circumstance is different. But in some cases, dealing with repeated affairs flung in your face is a form of emotional abuse and a definite lack of respect on the man's part. In the case of repeated indiscretions, forgiving him each time may signal the go-ahead for the next occurrence.

--*He's Just Being a Man*--

Sean Kelly, author of the magazine article "The Secret Life Of Men," puts the monogamous man in an unappealing light, referring to him as "an unvirile pill, a loveless leftover on the shelf." His assumption, a common one, is that monogamy can't possibly be satisfying for any man. Similar dribble reverberates in locker rooms across the country. A monogamous man is abnormal. If you're a real man and you don't chase tail, something's wrong with you. It takes a self-assured man to go against this societal grain, and more and more men are living up to the challenge. But wives and girlfriends have an unwritten code they also repeatedly follow. Many accept one or two flings as being the norm for a man. When a man enjoys an occasional sexual indiscretion, some women help reinforce the belief that he's just being a man.

Monogamy is coming back stronger than ever. Still, there are many men who believe a little bit of infidelity sparingly peppered throughout the marital years is O.K., and by accepting one or two flings as par for the course, many women help men perpetuate the behavior.

Is It Good for the Gander?

An unpleasant trend popping up with many men cheating, is women cheating on their men. Anthony P. Thompson, Ph.D, of the Western Australian Institute of Technology, alleges that upwards of 50% of married women have extramarital affairs. "If men can do it, so can we," remarked one woman. This kind of thinking falls in line with the old saying: If it's good for the goose, it's good for the gander.

The problem with that is cheating isn't good for *anybody*. It's a no-win situation. A woman caught cheating on her mate will probably muddle through the same shame, guilt, and remorse most men do. *Most men don't want to cheat.* The notion that a man cheats easily and with no conscience is, in most cases, a myth.

Once during a radio talk show interview I did with my husband, a man who had been unfaithful to his wife called in to talk about the remorse he experienced after his extramarital affair. He explained that he and his wife had sought counseling to deal with the hurt, shame, and anger. He said even though his wife has since healed and stopped going to counseling, he continues to go because he is having trouble dealing with his guilt. He regretfully acknowledged feeling that he can never rid himself of the feelings of remorse his infidelity has brought him. The trauma he put his family through proved almost too much for him or his marriage to bear. He is one of many men who suffer tremendous guilt after they cheat.

After the Affair

Though you can never turn back adulterous pages, you can go forward and deal with the situation. Many couples do decide to put the extramarital affair behind them and make their relationship work. It can be done and if both parties genuinely want the marriage to work, the results are worth the effort.

Most people are unprepared for the guilt and emotional trauma an affair brings about. If you do decide to stay together and work it out, expect a bumpy road. Also prepare to make some real changes. The authors of *The Dance-Away Lover* stress that if you do not make genuine changes in your intimate relationship, you will more than likely find the old problems resurfacing again in a year or two.

But I Love Him

He broke my heart. I could kill him for what he put me through. I hate what he did, but *I love him.* Shirley Pugh, a woman who started a support group in San Diego for wives of straying husbands, has heard similar words uttered many times. She says a woman should not feel like something is wrong with her if she wants to stay with her man after he has strayed. The American Association of Therapists affirms that 50% of marriages do survive infidelity. Pugh says that if the couple still love each other, they can build an even better relationship together. In the magazine article "Good Husbands Do Stray," marriage counselor Sonya Rhodes says that "many couples turn the crisis into an opportunity to build a better, more dynamic marriage."

Pugh states that many couples learn how to infidelity-proof their marriages after an affair. "The best way to do that is for both parties to work to rebuild all the bridges that broke down and lead him to wander." She contends that it's not easy, but a couple can recover from this crisis.

She is quick to caution women who are dealing with an unfaithful partner to expect feelings of anger and betrayal to linger for awhile. "He has to understand that what he did caused you an immense amount of pain. You need time to grieve and heal. You tolerated his extramarital escapade, now he must be tolerant of your feelings. You will have to work to rebuild your trust, and he will have to work hard to regain it."

Many women think that keeping the marriage intact after an extramarital affair means being and doing everything to please him, but Pugh says this is the wrong approach. "I advise women to take care of their own needs, and the rest will fall into place." Pugh feels that if you concentrate on his needs, he may view this as you chasing after him and think you are needy. "That can make him run right back to the other woman's arms," warns Pugh. She often attracts him because he sees her as independent and self-assured. She doesn't need him, she wants him. *To a man, that can make all the difference.* Pugh says that by going on with your life as if you can make it with or without him, you'll possess the qualities that draw him to the other woman.

This positive attitude also helps build your self-confidence. One woman managed to do such a complete job of standing on her own two feet that when her husband begged her to let him come home after he ended his fling, she didn't know if she wanted him back. Her newfound independence gave her a confidence she had never experienced.

With the crisis behind you, if you do decide to stay together or leave and eventually find another man, you don't ever want to face the ordeal of encountering another extramarital affair. You do, however, want to take your intimate relationship to a new plane. You can do that easily by discovering how indulging in a marital affair can put an arousing new face on your union.

The sweetest vindication I can think of for a woman who has suffered at the often cruel hands of the other woman is to go on to enjoy the richest and most rewarding intimate relationship she can. And what's best about enjoying a marital affair is that *the powers of the mistress become yours.*

Five

A Promise of Passion: The Marital Affair

"I Can't Have an Affair With You--I'm Your *Wife!*"

The marital affair breaks all the traditional rules. Marriage offers little excitement--the sensuality and enjoyment come *before* you walk down the aisle, while you're still dating each other. That's the only period in your relationship you have license to pant hotly after one another. Soon after you exchange your vows, the doldrums will move in and settle down for a long, comfortable stay. You never hear people referring to an old married couple as passionate lovers who can't keep their hands off each other. Lovers--that's a term reserved for people who are happily dating. Sexual hunger and fiery passion simply don't exist after marriage.

When my husband, Smitty, first suggested we have an affair, I briefly questioned the idea because I was thinking about the old rules. I reasoned that married people don't lust after each other. I'm the responsible wife; I can't be his mistress. But he persisted. His idea to enjoy a long-distance marital affair was born after he found out his military job was sending him to Iceland for one year, unaccompanied by me or our children.

My first husband, Arthur, was unfaithful even when we were sleeping in the same bed, so naturally, it crossed my mind that Smitty may find it difficult to remain monogamous while physically separated from me for an entire year. Once a man has cheated on you, the fear it may happen again, even with a different partner, isn't uncommon. And when you are a military spouse, you hear horror stories about how men in uniform go overseas and carry on yearlong wild, erotic parties with other women while separated from their families. I was honest with Smitty about my concerns.

He convincingly quieted my fears by telling me something I will never forget. It changed our marriage forever. Gently lifting my chin so I could look directly into his eyes, he cupped my hands in his and reassuringly told me, "I don't need to cheat on you." I could hear the conviction in his deep voice. "If I want to have an affair with someone, I can have one with you." My instantaneous reaction was, "I can't have an affair with you--I'm your wife!" However, Smitty's resolve encouraged me to give his idea serious thought. I also pondered marriage in general and those old rules.

Experts measure the divorce rate at over 51% today. That means more people split up than stay together. I determined that if we followed the normal path of other twosomes, we could face a 50/50 chance of survival. That's when I decided to explore my husband's inviting concept and put the marital odds more in our favor. Little did we know that our long-distance liaison would turn into a lifelong commitment of a partnership filled with love, passion, and the kind of fiery sexual desire most couples leave at the altar.

My husband's determination to make a firm commitment to monogamy, even in the face of a long separation did a lot for both of us, and his idea to embark on a marital affair changed our relationship 100% for the better. We wrote each other "for your eyes only" love letters almost daily and called each other weekly. We called ourselves secret lovers, our affair known only to us. After he returned from his yearlong duty in Iceland, we went on a cruise to renew our newfound fervor for each other. That entire year we created memories that will last us a lifetime. It has been many years since we started our marital affair, and we've continued creating those same kind of love-filled remembrances ever since. Our affair brings us closer together everyday.

You Are Already Having an Affair

If you and your significant other have a loving relationship, you already have the beginnings of a marital affair. The definition of *affair* is, no less, *an amorous relationship between two people.* The word affair has been tainted because people associate it with extramarital affair. Let's look at what's wrong with the extramarital affair. You have two people involved in an exhilarating, often loving relationship--what is wrong with that? Absolutely nothing. What *is* wrong with the extramarital affair is that the two people engaging in it do not belong together. Their stolen moments of happiness are at someone else's expense.

The marital affair is also a loving relationship, but replacing the word *extramarital* with *marital* makes all the difference. By enjoying your affair together, you live out the fantasy of engaging in a private, sensual love affair, and no one gets hurt in the process. The marital affair offers you the best of both worlds. It includes the same sweltering passion the extramarital affair holds for men and women who are looking to revive their routine sex life, but it does not hold the risk an extramarital affair does. It makes sense for a couple to look for passion, love, and excitement in their own backyard.

Strengthening Your Marital Chain

A strong marriage or intimate relationship is like a solidly built chain-link fence. One broken link can expose the entire fence.

The first secret:

> The other woman looks to expose weak links in your marital chain.

The other woman has no effect on a happy marriage. She looks for signs that spell trouble in paradise. Throughout this book, I will uncover areas where your intimate relationship may become vulnerable. Just like the fence, one broken link that goes unfixed leads to another. Pretty soon, the entire fence comes down under the weight of too many broken links. Understanding the "weak link" concept will take you a long way in keeping your marital fence standing tall--undaunted by the other woman. *One of the strongest links you can have in your fence is the marital affair.*

Putting the Marriage Odds in Your Favor

If a banker encouraged you to invest $500 in his bank but you faced a 50/50 chance of losing your money, would you invest? Would you accept a job promotion knowing there was a 50/50 chance the department you will transfer to may close down in a year? Those are high odds--gambling odds. With the divorce rate over 51% that means staying together forever only counts in 49% of marriages. What can you do? Cross your fingers and hope for the best? Like when you pull the one-arm bandit of a slot machine in Vegas, praying for three lucky sevens every time?

We all want to be happy in life, and we deserve that happiness. We *can* change the marriage odds. Relationships today are no different from ones of a generation ago. You still have two people who want to spend a lifetime of happiness together. When Helen Gurley Brown, editor of *Cosmopolitan Magazine,* describes the man-woman relationship as "the most important thing in our lives," she is right. If your intimate relationship is unhealthy, it has a negative affect on everything you do. In a study about depression, conducted by George Brown and Tirril Harris, findings showed that strong marital relations influence the psychological well-being of both partners.

How can you make sure your marriage is solid, and how can you make sure your relationship with your spouse will last forever? While there are no guarantees, you can reach beyond the typical marriage and work to create a union that promises to be as rewarding and stimulating as you want it to be. The marital affair helps put the odds in your favor because it puts your union a spark above the average one.

Too many couples slip into matrimony like a comfortable pair of shoes they hastily toss aside when the road they travel gets tough. A marital affair is different because it is a driving commitment to a lifelong liaison of happiness and fulfillment for both of you. It can be added to your bond to rekindle over and over the electricity that raced through your veins when you two first met.

A marital affair doesn't replace the traditional relationship between man and wife. Instead, you add it to your intimate bond to remind you to keep the romance blossoming. When a man or woman has a thrilling extramarital affair, one commonality it offers them is: **ESCAPE.** This escape can be from a myriad of circumstances including the grind of everyday life, a boring sex life, or an inattentive mate. There is nothing wrong with seeking an outlet from life's pressures, as long as it's healthy. That's what the marital affair offers both of you, a healthy escape from the routine that traditional marriage lends itself to.

A marital affair is like a classic movie. It's not something you want to indulge in everyday because that will make its magic average and ordinary. Instead, it's something you want to use now and again to turn the routine into something exciting and wonderful. One element many people who engage in extramarital affairs cite as enticing is the secrecy of meeting their lovers in hotel rooms and secluded restaurants. The marital affair offers you the chance to do the same, but without the dire consequences of an extramarital affair. What could be more arousing than a clandestine meeting with your spouse as your date? Both of you can steal a few moments to stop worrying about everyday hassles and enjoy being together as passionate lovers.

As one married mistress's husband put it, "It gives you permission to move back to the romance you let fall by the wayside." He goes on to emphasize how essential an ingredient the marital affair is to his marriage. "I get to have the most exciting affair of my dreams--and I get to enjoy the fantasy with my wife! What more can a guy ask for?" Another man says having a marital affair with his married mistress means never having a dull moment. "I never know what she has in store for us," he grins.

Other men and women who have taken the Married Mistress or Monogamous Male Seminar share what having a marital affair does for their intimate relationships:

> ♥ It's full of excitement
> ♥ It's like dating a bunch of different guys--I have
>   multiple lovers in one body
> ♥ It's spontaneous
> ♥ It prevents romance from becoming routine
> ♥ It positively affects everything you do
> ♥ It offers a fresh approach and different perspective
> ♥ It opens sensitivity to one another
> ♥ It keeps us in love *and in lust* with each other.

To reap all the benefits of what a marital affair promises, we first need to discover the temptation behind the extramarital affair. You'll find there are many positive elements you can take from the extramarital affair and put to good use in your marital affair. The next chapter bares all about what happens between a married man and the other woman in their forbidden rendezvous.

Six

What *Really* Goes on in Extramarital Affairs

"First of all, we don't have unlimited sex!" She strongly emphasized that point between puffs of her cigarette. "Mind you, the sex is good, but that's not all that goes on." It was a rainy day when I interviewed Sally who proudly referred to herself as a "kept woman."

The bright, red lipstick she wore stained the tip of her cigarette. Her quiet, unassuming appearance was not anything like I pictured while conversing with her over the telephone. She was short and stocky and looked to be in her forties. The rain had matted her bangs to her forehead. Her long, straight hairstyle reminded me of an afghan's coat--long and stringy. Sally bragged about what she thinks she does best: "I date my best friends' husbands."

She went on to tell me how easy it is to fool one of her friends. "I just pretend I like her kids. I come around all the time. Pretty soon, she starts leaving me with them and her husband while she runs errands. Sometimes, we start having sex right there in her bed. Most of the time, the wives never even have a clue." She laughed then continued. "They're just glad to have someone watch the kids and give them a break. If they only knew what I do when I baby-sit their kids."

I finally steered her towards talking about her long-term affairs. "Oh, well I did get involved with a couple of my friends' husbands for a long time. So you want to know what really goes on." After a lengthy pause, she inhaled a deep puff of her second cigarette, blew it up towards the ceiling and continued. "We had great sex for the first couple of months. We did it anywhere, in hotel rooms, in their bedrooms, at my house. But, you know, after a while, the sex gets boring. The man I dated the longest? We were together about two years. And like I was saying, we got to the place where the sex wasn't even important. Sometimes, he'd rent a hotel room for a whole weekend; he told his wife he had out-of-town business," she grinned, "and we'd only have sex once. The rest of the time, we just talked."

I had similar conversations with other women who sleep with married men. Most of them agreed that in long-term affairs with attached men, sex plays a surprisingly small role. The sexual magnetism may be what starts the extramarital liaison, but, in many cases, it's not what sustains a long term one.

Why Men Cheat

Many wives believe husbands cheat mainly to fulfill an animalistic need for sex. However, in *The McGill Report On Male Intimacy,* author Michael McGill paints us a different picture: "A more common problem may be a man's *friendship* with other women. Often in these relationships a man discloses the very intimacies that he withholds from his wife." When we look for someone to blame, it's easy for us to point to the man who strayed or the woman who wooed him. Though the part they play is wrong and hurtful, it's important to do what the mistress advised earlier, look at the part a wife can play in this triangle. If wives don't look to their part, they end up cheating themselves because refusing to acknowledge past mistakes leaves the possibility of repeating them.

If his uncontrollable libido isn't the driving force that causes him to temporarily lose his sanity and commit the heinous crime of adultery, what makes a man risk everything he has taken the time to build with his mate for this friendship with another woman? The following are some of the most common reasons men stray:

> • **Lack of Attention**
> --Forgetting Your First Child--
> • **A Need to Fantasize or Realize a Dream**
> • **Lack of Intimacy**
> • **Sexual Hunger**
> --The Madonna Complex--
> • **Narcissism**
> • **Midlife Crisis**
> • **Chronic Boredom**

Lack of Attention

I discovered a difference in the way men and women prioritize their love partners while watching one of my favorite game shows, Wheel Of Fortune. Pat Sajack, the show's host, usually encourages each contestant to tell a little about themselves. I noticed that often, a married woman's reply is similar to the following:

> "Well Pat, I have two lovely children, Sarah and John, Jr., ages eight and four, hi kids!" She grins into the television camera while excitedly waving. "I attend night classes, I'm training to be a nurse, I work part-time as a sales representative, and I'd like to say hi to Sue and Linda at the office. I have an aunt, uncle, three cousins, a dog, two hamsters..."

"That's fine, Pat interrupts so he can move on to the next guest. But before he does, Cindy suddenly remembers who she left out. "Oh, Pat," she hurriedly squeezes in, "I forgot about my husband, John. He's out in the audience."

That's what I refer to as *the Wheel of Misplaced Fortune*. It happens when a woman puts everything and everyone before her intimate relationship and her mate. The typical response from the married male contestant is to mention his wife first. Sometimes, men will mention their wives second after their jobs, but that's another book.

A common complaint from men who stray is that their wives stop paying attention to them. Just like the spouse in the game show, many women go from putting their significant others first to putting them last on their Wheels, especially after the children arrive.

"She used to be so attentive," shares one man who's been dating other women for over eight of his fifteen years of marriage. "But she became too busy raising our children. We never spend time alone anymore. We haven't been out without the kids in years, and I gave up trying a long time ago."

One man who walked out on his wife after twenty-five years told me he left because she neglected him to raise the children. "Nancy's priority has been motherhood from the first day she gave birth to Timothy. Our sex life definitely took a back seat, though I honestly don't think Nancy ever even noticed. If she did notice, she didn't care. She was always going on about the big responsibility we had to the kids. We had to be the perfect role models. If you're wondering if I told Nancy how I felt, I did--over and over. I tried not to be angry when I complained, and after awhile, I complained less and less. When I told her how I felt, she just didn't pay attention."

Experts agree that, unfortunately, many women turn to their children for love and nurturing while simultaneously turning away from their mates. In their book depicting *American Couples*, Dr. Philip Blumstein and Dr. Pepper Swartz say that children have a big impact on marital relationships. They affirm that this impact can be an unhappy one on husbands who find that the children sometimes interfere with their sex lives and affection from their spouses.

While you were dating him, your relationship took precedence over everything else. Being together was your main mission. Many men expect that to continue after matrimony. They don't want to put the intimacy on the back burner, but sometimes when a woman gets involved with motherhood, her career, and other outside interests she can become unknowingly neglectful. This is not to say the same thing doesn't happen to a man. One man told me he and his wife were both guilty of putting their children before the marriage: "It got to the point we both enjoyed being with the kids more than being with each other. I believe that attitude contributed a lot to our divorce."

Raising children is one of the hardest yet most rewarding jobs a couple will ever tackle. It's time consuming and never ending, and it's a job many parents, especially mothers, can innocently get lost in. It's essential, however, that both of you remember what came first-- *you and him.* The intimate partnership you formed brought about your children. It's up to both of you to work at keeping the romance alive. Nurture your liaison together just like you would another child.

--Forgetting Your First Child--

It's the seed that started it all. Your happy home and beautiful children are the direct result of the love you share for one another. Take care not to leave your seed untended. Could you even imagine a mother who would turn her back on one child to raise another? Society would condemn her. Yet, that same woman can get away with turning her back on her intimate relationship to raise her new child. When she turns around eighteen years later to pick up where she left off, she often finds her man long gone. Someone else picked up the pieces for her. And she'll usually blame her husband for not being able to keep his pants on instead of acknowledging the part she played in the triangle.

The female Octopus has an interesting way to nurture her young. After the male impregnates her, she fiercely guards her eggs for the four to eight week period it takes for them to hatch. She constantly cleans them with her suckers and agitates them with water every few seconds. Oh, by the way, while she's doing all this work for her eggs, the male Octopus goes on his merry way, looking to mate with another female Octopus (sounds like another species some of us know). The female Octopus puts her life into protecting her eggs. While she agitates them, she does nothing else. She doesn't sleep, doesn't eat, she just blows on her precious eggs every few seconds. Soon after the eggs hatch, the female Octopus usually dies from starvation. She gives her life for her young.

You're probably saying that comparing humans to an Octopus is a little ridiculous. After all, as human females we are a lot smarter than that. Well, look at how many mothers stop living their lives and start living vicariously through their young. And when their children grow up and leave, they feel lost. Why? Because they give their lives to their young. They let a little of themselves go to raise them. Oftentimes, one part of themselves they let go of is their intimate relationship. Just like the female Octopus, the intimate relationship dies a slow death--from starvation. You have to feed your relationship just like you would another child.

Raise your children. Give them all the love and support they need. Nurture your career and family ties. They are important to you. Just remember your first child--the seed you planted together, *your marriage*. Give it as much love and support as you give any of your children. After all, your goal is to stay together as a family. That means being happy as a couple.

A Need to Fantasize or Realize a Dream

Harry is what many women consider an attractive catch. He owns a successful company, is a faithful husband, and he balances his work and home life well. He's a handsome man with a long, taut physique. He has a well-groomed mustache, and at forty-six, his full head of hair shows an attractive pattern of just a touch of gray at the temples. Harry says he's very content with his life, but this wasn't always so.

"I married Kate right out of high school. I've always wanted to own a trucking company, but I put off my dream to pay bills and provide for my family. When the kids got older, I tried to tell Kate about my dream to run my own business. But, whenever I mentioned it, she reacted negatively. She told me I could never own my own company because we couldn't afford it and I didn't know anything about running a business. Anyway, she said we needed to be practical. After awhile, whenever I approached her with the idea she'd get angry. I finally got up the courage to go to business school. That's where I met Sarah. We didn't start having an affair right away. At first, she was just someone to listen to my ideas. But she encouraged me. She said I could own a trucking company if I really wanted to. Sarah made me believe in myself. When I made up my mind to go into business, I also made another big move in my life. I left my wife and married Sarah. Now I own my own trucking company and Sarah runs the office. I'm not saying our divorce was all my ex-wife's fault. I know I'm not perfect. I didn't mean to have an affair; we were married for over seventeen years before I cheated on her. But I had to live out my dream, and when she didn't believe in me, I just couldn't face up to that. I needed to be with someone who believed in me. Kate tells all her friends I left her for another woman, but there is so much more to it than that. The marriage really ended when I realized how little Kate believed in me."

Sometimes a man's need to realize a dream brings him and his mistress together. If Harry's first wife had let him try his hand at starting a business, what would she have lost? Today, he's running a very successful company. She could have sat down with him and talked out an agreement. He could have set aside so much of his income for the business, or he could have worked a part-time job to get the money. Instead, she let her fear of failure fog her judgement, and that made the subject unapproachable to her. Her determination to stifle his dream cost her much more than a temporary inconvenience. It eventually was the catalyst that helped to end their marriage. It's important for both you and your mate to have the chance to realize your hopes and dreams. Nobody likes their dreams discounted by anybody, especially a loved one.

Lack of Intimacy

As Michael McGill confirmed earlier, the most threatening type of affair your man can have with another woman is not a sexual one, but an intimate one. While sex usually plays a small role, intimacy can play a dangerously more important one. McGill explains that the real threat to a wife is not the woman her husband just has sexual relations with. When a husband's interconnection with the other woman becomes so close that he shares the dimensions of him he cannot or will not share with his mate, that entanglement is the one that poses the most threat to the marriage.

"I married Jane after having an affair with her for over five years. Alice and I had a very nasty divorce. After she found out I was seeing Jane, she said I was just a horny bastard who couldn't get enough. The funny thing about Jane and me is that most of the time we were together, we didn't even have sex. We talked--about everything."

At forty-three, Stanley, a mechanic, says he'd been unhappy with his marriage to his wife, Alice, for years. He explained that the main reason he left Alice for Jane was because he was able to divulge his most intimate secrets, his hopes, and fears to her without fear of rejection. "With Jane I can fail. I can cry and not have to be strong all the time. There was no room for any of that with Alice. Sure, I played tough guy when we were dating, but it was a role she never let me stop playing. I guess I just got tired. Whenever I tried to show Alice I was hurt or upset about something, she couldn't handle it. Even when she encouraged me to express my feelings, when I did she'd say I was just being weak or she'd call me a wimp. She even got angry once when I cried after our dog got ran over. It hurt me to see my children cry, but she said they needed me to be strong. Well I am strong, but I'm also sensitive. I can share my most intimate thoughts with Jane and not worry that she'll use them as ammo against me like Alice always did."

Not giving your man comfortable ground to share his innermost thoughts and fears can be dangerous. It can leave a huge hole in your intimate relationship--one the other woman is usually more than eager to fill. In a study of extramarital involvement in the *Journal of Sex Research*, John Edwards says that often when the husband confides in the other woman, that serves as a common starting point for infidelity.

Sexual Hunger

While it's important for a wife to understand the role she can play in her husband's infidelity, it's also important to note that sometimes a man's cheating ways have nothing to do with his wife. No matter how attentive their mates are, some men will always cheat. Their sexual appetites or overblown egos can't be satisfied by one woman. At least, that's what they believe. These men are usually habitual strayers. "The Don Juan Syndrome," a magazine article penned by Neil Chesanow identifies men who routinely cheat as womanizers. Some famous Don Juans include Donald Trump, Warren Beatty, Clark Gable, and John Barrymore. These men have all been well documented as womanizers.

Chesanow reveals that many of these men, who seem to be in control on the surface, usually court very fragile egos. Oftentimes, their insecurity leads them to have non-committal liaisons with woman after woman, never allowing themselves to fully commit to one. Even when they marry they continue justifying this destructive behavior. Some of these men run from commitment because they are afraid of being hurt by a woman.

Interestingly enough, many womanizer's drives aren't sexual in nature, they often enjoy the thrill of the hunt more. These men chase as many skirts as they can. Their enjoyment comes from the racy and dangerous excitement they get in dangling as many women as they can on a string.

Habitual straying is often a learned behavior. Jim, an air force officer, says many of his military colleagues sleep around on their wives when they go out of town on business. The military often sends men and women in uniform to remote job assignments without their families. These assignments can last anywhere from a few weeks to a couple of years. Jim says when he asks these men why they are unfaithful, most of them say their dad had affairs, or they saw their brothers sleeping around on their wives or girlfriends. Jim disagrees with his colleagues who cheat because he feels he has too much to lose. He also sees the guilt his fellow officers suffer. He says it's much more pleasing to him to have an affair with his wife. She attended one of the first Married Mistress Seminars.

What can you do if you are in love with a man who suffers from the Don Juan Syndrome? First recognize *you are not the source of the problem*. If you are doing everything to keep your relationship fulfilling and he continues to cheat, you have to do some serious soul searching. Both of you can seek marriage counseling. If your man refuses to get help, you have to ask yourself if you continually want to deal with having extramarital affairs painfully hurled at you. You must decide if you want to repeatedly deal with this emotionally draining predicament or if you want to leave and find someone who won't forfeit the bankroll of trust you put into them.

--The Madonna Complex--

Sexual hunger manifests itself in yet another way that can prove very harmful to a marriage. The Madonna Complex creates conflict in the way some men view their wives. This complex occurs when a man sees his wife as a nice girl who doesn't engage in gratifying sex. In her excellent study of *Men Who Can't Be Faithful,* Carol Botwin notes that Elvis Presley suffered from what she terms the Pedestal/Gutter Syndrome. She says after he married Priscilla, who was a virgin when they met, he lost sexual interest in her and began sleeping with women who he didn't respect, but who excited him physically.

One woman, whose husband felt strongly about her not indulging in lustful sex, said she found out (after he died) he had been secretly sleeping with prostitutes and other women to live out sexual fantasies he viewed as too lewd for his wife to carry out. She attempted to get him to change his attitude by tempting him with sensual lingerie, but he chastised her calling her a whore and slut. She said it shocked her to find out her husband was fulfilling fantasies he called sinful with other women and had been throughout their twenty-seven years of marriage. She admits that his staid attitude denied her of a gratifying sexual life. And all the while, he was enjoying sex with the wrong women when they could have been enjoying it together. He was unwilling to let his wife satisfy his innate hunger for sex, yet he was not about to let his sexual appetite go unfed.

There is no such thing as married sex. However, there *is* such a thing as lifeless sex. When people confuse natural sexual acts as off limits for marrieds, the results are often disastrous.

A man suffering from the Madonna Complex can often put his marriage in jeopardy unless he seeks counseling or therapy. A reputable sex therapist can assist men who suffer from this sexual dysfunction.

Narcissism

Love And Betrayal is a television movie in which actor David Birney plays a narcissist. A narcissist is a person who is so selfishly wrapped up in his own needs and wants, he automatically expects the same from others around him.

In the movie Birney walks out on his wife, played by Stephanie Powers, of twenty-five years to move in with a younger woman. Throughout the film, he keeps his wife's hopes dangling by not filing for divorce, by temporarily moving back home, and by keeping a key to the house to use whenever it suits him. It is his wife who finally takes a stand and asks him for a divorce. He's content having her and his mistress pining for him and waiting for him to decide what he wants.

In his best-seller, *The Culture Of Narcissism,* Christopher Lasch accuses this type of man of being a self-interested taker. The word *give* is not in his vocabulary. A narcissistic man is so self-involved, it rarely occurs to him that his self-serving actions may be ripping out someone's soul. Like the husband in the movie, a narcissist only wants what's best for him--even if it's at his wife's expense. It's not unusual for this type of man to be unfaithful.

A woman involved with a narcissist may have little recourse available to her but to do what Stephanie Powers' character did in the movie--decide her needs are as important as his. In this situation, a wife is not really competing with another woman, she is rivaling the narcissist's overblown ego. Rather than having eyes for another woman, the narcissist only has eyes for himself.

Midlife Crisis

Many extramarital affairs occur during a man's midlife crisis. For many people, midlife serves as a rude awakening that the clock is steadily ticking. Many men feel life has passed them by, and they try to recapture their youth by doing things that make them feel young. If a man has been a family man most of his adult life, one of those options may include having a midlife fling. Dr. Judith Kuriansky says men who feel this urge need to ask themselves if this fling is worth risking their marriages.

If you sense your man is going through a midlife crisis, Kuriansky has some suggestions. In her book about *Sex,* Kuriansky suggests you ride out the crisis by communicating with your mate. Try to understand and empathize with what he is going through. Listen to his feelings. She also suggests couples change their routine, relive their first date, and surprise each other. Thus, get back to romance. Often a man's urge to have a midlife fling is really a thinly disguised wish to recapture the romance he enjoyed with his mate when they first met.

Chronic Boredom

The final reason many men stray has to do with marital boredom. The marital doldrums can bring you and your man face-to-face with an experience of the most dulling kind, causing you to enter a zone more threatening to your happy home than the infamous twilight zone. There is no escaping it. Every relationship reaches a certain level of comfort--it's inevitable. You can expect a certain amount of boredom to intrude on your intimate relationship every now and then, but the danger comes when the boredom becomes chronic. Chronic boredom can lead your relationship into treacherous waters. The possibility lives in every relationship, waiting to strike at any moment. It creeps between your bed sheets at night and envelopes you. Or it can seep through the corners of your mate's comfortable armchair, holding him firmly in a vice-like grip. Turn the page to find out how your relationship can avoid...

Seven

The Comfort Zone

Happily Ever After

Remember when you two first met? He may not have been the most handsome man in the place, but there was something about him. The way his eyes nervously smiled at you, his shy grin, or maybe it was his gentle manner. The same thing that drew you to him caused stomach flurries whenever you thought of him.

What about your first date? You spent hours picking out just the right outfit, trying on dress after dress. The way you had shoes thrown everywhere and clothes strewn over the bed and chair made your room look like it had been in the path of a tornado. You finally found the most delicious outfit, guaranteed to knock his socks off. You put on your makeup like an artist painting her most delicate and precious piece of work, and you brushed your hair until it shimmered. Everything had to be perfect because you were going out with *him*. He took your emotions to places they had never visited--you didn't know what he did to you, but you knew you wanted that feeling to last forever. Your courtship was like a fond remembrance of your favorite fairy tale, with him as your handsome and attentive knight in shining armor. You wanted the romance to last a lifetime.

Then he proposed. Once you came down off your cloud, you started believing life really is going to be good to you. You said to yourself, "If this is a dream, please don't wake me up, yet." You took your vows, and when the preacher said, "To love and cherish," you knew you'd feel this way *forever*.

But now, with a few bills, kids, and mortgages playing interference, you wonder when your stomach flurries disappeared. When you look at your knight in shining armor these days, all you see is a receding hairline, pot-belly, and a man who likes to get it on every other Friday night.

You look at him planted in front of the TV watching his favorite football teams, the Raiders and Cowboys, battle their opponents on two opposite channels. The couch has attached itself to his behind, and his arm is about to grow a remote control any minute. He lets loose a loud belch while feeling for his second beer on the coffee table, his eyes still firmly glued to the set. You wonder where the man is who used to lift weights and looked so good when he came to pick you up for a date. Your mind even tricks you into smelling the aroma of his sexy cologne--*HUNK*; he used to smell so enticing. You quickly snap back to the present, however, when you walk into the bedroom and see his underwear flung inside out on the floor--no sexy aroma coming from there.

When you go to use the bathroom, you can't help but notice his trademark--the toilet seat is up again. Just before you close the bathroom door, you hear him in the living room letting another mammoth belch escape his beer belly. You sigh as you think about that short lifetime of romance.

And who does he see when he looks at you? The woman who takes care of his kids and has dinner on the table at six every night. He also sees a woman who gets up at seven in the morning, one hour before the kids wake up, so she can meticulously prepare her makeup and pick the right business outfit. He sees a woman who wants to look good on her job, but when she comes home, she can't wait to strip off her makeup and clothes and get comfortable in her tattered, blah-gray sweats.

You used to get gussied up for him, but now when you turn in at night he doesn't know whether your face color is going to be flesh-tone or avocado green. It depends on what night treatment you're trying out so you can look attractive at the office. He remembers the sexy black teddy and Chanel No. 5 he bought for your last birthday. You used to look and smell so good when you put on your silky lingerie and dabbed some sexy smelling cologne behind your ears. Now when you turn in he doesn't know whether you're going to smell like cucumbers or rubbing alcohol. He just knows that he doesn't smell Chanel No. 5 anymore. He remembers you nonchalantly thanking him for the birthday gifts while looking at them like you really wanted something else, then he never saw them again. He sighs as he remembers that every night you cuddle up to your flannel night gown, not to him. He wonders, like you, why the romance and excitement fizzled so quickly.

Any of that sound remotely familiar? If it does--welcome to the Comfort Zone. It's the difference between being at ease in your intimate relationship and being chronically bored with each other. It's almost like being in a coma--a marital coma. Both of you settle into everyday life and slowly let your romance die out. It's not unusual-- and it happens at different times in every intimate relationship. There's no escaping it. What's important about the Comfort Zone is recognizing it and getting out of it.

Is Your Relationship in the Comfort Zone?

In your Married Mistress Workbook (see page 15), circle the answer that most closely fits your relationship now.

1. How often do you go out to dinner or out on the town? (Just the two of you.)
   a) Once or twice a month.
   b) Once or twice every other month.
   c) Once or twice every six months.
   d) We rarely go out without the children.

2. How often do you have sex?
   a) Three to four times a week.
   b) Once a week.
   c) Once a month.
   d) Less than once a month.

3. How often do the two of you sit and talk? (Arguments don't count.)
   a) Everyday.
   b) Two or three times a week.
   c) Once a week.
   d) Not frequently. Just whenever we get a free moment, which isn't often.

4. You go on a romantic holiday or an overnighter together,
   a) Once a month.
   b) Once a year.
   c) Once every two to three years.
   d) We don't go on vacations without the children.

5. How often do you say I love you to each other?

a) Daily.
b) Once or twice a week.
c) Less than once or twice a week.
d) Occasionally.
e) I don't remember the last time we said I love you to each other.

6. How often do you cuddle and hug each other?
   a) We just can't keep our hands off each other.
   b) Frequently.
   c) Occasionally.
   d) Not very often.

7. How often do you watch TV or enjoy another leisure activity *together?*
   a) Everyday.
   b) Three to four times a week.
   c) Once or twice weekly.
   d) He has his leisure activities--I have mine.

8. How often do you argue?
   a) Less than once or twice a week.
   b) Two to three times a week.
   c) Three to four times a week.
   d) More than three to four times a week.
   e) That's the only time we talk.

9. You've just been given an extra hour a week. Out of these four choices, which one would you pick to fill that time?
   a) Making love.
   b) Spending it with my mate doing whatever we enjoy.
   c) Reading a romance novel.
   d) Watching my favorite soap opera.

   If you answered A or B to these questions, *congratulations.* Your relationship is at a safe level of comfort--you just need to work at keeping it there. However, recognizing the Comfort Zone is still important because when your relationship does saunter into it, you can take steps to revive your romance.
   If you answered C, D, or E to any of these questions, the two of you may be venturing into the Comfort Zone.

Getting Out of the Marital Rut

For most couples, the hardest part of getting out of the Comfort Zone is realizing they are in it. The marital coma becomes so commonplace that years can go by before a couple realizes their union is in danger. Oftentimes, couples don't face this problem until it's too late. One woman, who took the Married Mistress Seminar, admitted that she and her husband had been in the Comfort Zone for years but they didn't recognize it. When she finally did acknowledge the relationship was in trouble, she didn't know what to do--so she didn't do anything. After fifteen years of marriage, her husband left her for another woman. She says she knows now that a relationship takes work from both partners and says she is learning her skills *before* she experiences trouble in her next relationship.

Susan says she took the seminar because she and her husband were getting into a rut. At the end of the first class, the homework assignment was for each woman to go home and do something special for her love partner. Susan stopped at a convenience mart and bought her husband a beautiful, blood-red rose. "When he came home and saw the rose on his pillow," she excitedly told the class the following week, "he hugged me and kissed me on the cheek. At first I was tempted to tell him I was taking a cooking class because I didn't know how he'd feel about me taking a relationship course, but I was honest and told him I signed up for the Married Mistress Seminar. He was so impressed. That night, we talked for a long time. He told me how glad he was I decided to start working on our relationship. He admitted he thought we were in a rut but didn't know how to tell me. I'm glad I followed my instincts. Next week, we're going on a romantic getaway--just the two of us."

The worst thing you can do when you sense your partnership is too comfortable is nothing. If Susan had ignored the signs, she and Don would still be silently going along, knowing their union was suffering from a lack of romance. The minute she made a move, he followed her lead to recreate the atmosphere they enjoyed. Susan took steps to get her marriage out of the Comfort Zone making, her union with Don even stronger.

Another remedy for getting out of a martial rut is learning to look at your relationship in a new light. Or I should say an old, familiar one.

Five Steps to Getting Out of the Comfort Zone

♦ Acknowledge it. One of the most crucial steps to getting out of a marital rut is realizing you are in it.

♦ Admit to it. It doesn't matter whether it is you or your partner. One of you needs to say, "We're in a rut, and we need to get out."

♦ Don't react negatively. This applies to both of you. If your mate says you are in the Comfort Zone, listen--don't react angrily. He shouldn't get offended if you are the one to acknowledge the rut.

♦ Do something! This is crucial. Once you acknowledge the Comfort Zone, take swift action to reverse the situation.

♦ Be on the lookout. Make a pact with your partner that either of you can acknowledge your marital rut without an angry reaction from the other.

Eight

Old Eyes Versus New Ones

One of the first exercises in the Married Mistress Seminar consists of having attendees examine how they look at their love partners. Through this exercise, more than one woman discovers when she first met her mate, the eyes she looked at him with found the true beauty of her man. Those eyes concentrated on everything she loved about him and saw her special relationship with her mate as one rich in love and laughter.

As time wears on, however, a woman sometimes trades that pair of eyes for a new pair of sharper, more critical ones. With these new eyes, rather than focusing on what she loves about him, she begins examining her mate's faults more closely. The trick for a woman who looks at her love partner with these new eyes is to make the old seem new again. To do that, she must replace her new, fault-finding eyes with the old pair of loving eyes that brought the two of them together.

The New Pair of Eyes

In the first part of this exercise seminar attendees discuss what they dislike about their mates. Their responses are always interesting:

"My husband makes it all the way to the clothes hamper, but he drops his dirty clothes on the floor, directly in front of the hamper instead of inside. That drives me crazy," shared one married mistress.

"Mine leaves little pieces of toothpaste plastered on the mirror after he brushes his teeth," quipped another. "I feel like I'm always cleaning up behind him in the bathroom."

Sharon frantically raised her hand so she could speak next. "My boyfriend's snoring is about to drive me to drink! Sometimes I feel like hitting him in the head with my pillow, or a rock! I can't sleep when he snores!"

After a few moments of keenly focusing on their mates' faults, it's time to steer the women to the point of the exercise: learning to refocus their energies on positive qualities. But before we move to phase two of this exercise, I make it clear that it's not unusual for them to dislike certain bad habits their partners may possess. I don't ask the women to discount these annoyances. When their love partners do things that disturb them, like leaving the bathroom untidy, for instance, they need to openly discuss the problem with their mates.

Learning to respect each other's needs and differences takes a lot of communication and patience, as well as give and take from both partners. A good part of patience comes into play when we learn not to hone in on the negatives. Constantly zeroing in on his bad habits while forgetting to weigh those irritants against what you admire about your love mate will force you to see him in an uninteresting, even aggravating light.

A sure-fire cure for putting what bugs you about your mate into proper perspective is to look at him in a light you may have forgotten about. It's the same enthusiastic light that brought you two together.

The Old Pair of Eyes

When asked to share what first attracted them to their mates, it takes most of the seminar attendees a few moments to shift gears from their negative thoughts. Here's what some of them shared:

"I fell in love with his sexy baby-blues." Marilyn's eyes glazed over while she drifted into a dream-like state.

"His buns," laughed Susan. "He has the greatest butt."

"I love his hairy chest," said Linda. "Sometimes I like to run my fingers through all those manly hairs." She quivered at the thought of her sexy husband.

"Steve can be so romantic sometimes," shared Tammy. "One time when I was feeling a little down on myself, I don't know why, I just did. Anyway, Steve rented a limousine to take me out to dinner.

And he actually had the driver give me a dozen roses! I'll never forget how wonderful he made me feel that night--he made me feel so very special." Tammy was nearly in tears.

The transformation that overtook these women when they focused on the positives was dramatic. Their taut and tense shoulders began to relax, and a peaceful, dreamy gaze replaced the intense look some of them had on their faces as they began to remember *why they fell in love.*

Sometimes You Need to Put Those Rose Colored Glasses Back On

A major part of enjoying a rewarding marital affair lies in the ability to remember what brought the two of you together. What caused your heart to do a flip-flop dance when you were dating him? What made you pick him? He possessed something special that made you select him over your other suitors. You chose him to share in a lifetime of loving.

When we are madly in love, we tend to see a vision of our beau that may be a bit colored. So in all the years of living with him you discover he can't walk on water after all. You see his striking blue eyes get red from tiredness, and you even realize that, occasionally, he's afraid of failure. He's vulnerable to life's ups and downs, he makes mistakes, and he has some bad habits. Just like you, he's human.

That doesn't mean now and then you can't put those rose colored glasses back on and reflect on your fond memories of when you two were dating and relive those special moments. In fact, it's essential because you never want to forget the real beauty and uniqueness of your mate. By making it a point to remember why you picked him, you'll never let go of the special attraction you hold for him.

Life Without Him

The more romantic and happy moments you create together, the bigger your positive memory bank becomes. The more positives you have to feed on, the less you will dwell on negative thoughts. This positive memory bank is what both of you will draw from whenever times get tough.

There's another important aspect to creating romantic, everlasting memories. An enlightening way to put your mate's irritating habits into perspective is to imagine life without him. Pretend you've separated, divorced, or he died. He's no longer a part of your life, and you know you'll *never* see him again.

How important are those little irritants now? How important do you think those messy bathroom habits will be? If he snores, will you long to hear that sound again because at least it means he's sleeping next to you? Will you think about him when you see the tube of toothpaste never has the top missing anymore?

I received a heavy-hearted call from a listener once during a television interview. She wanted to know how to begin the dating process again after being a widow for over eleven years. Life suddenly yanked her husband from her when he died one night in a car accident. At the time, she was in her early thirties.

She said that more than anything, she wished she could have her husband back. However, she realized he will never be with her again so she reluctantly wanted to know how to begin looking for someone new. I talked with her over the telephone for almost forty-five minutes, long after the television show ended, and the crew had disappeared off the set. In all that time, she talked about her man and their life together. She didn't talk about the little things he did that rode her nerves. All this lonely woman could remember about her mate is what is really important--*the love he left behind.*

The Love Stays With You

The average woman outlives her husband by seven years. Unfortunately, many women may one day face the possibility of outliving their mates. That's another reason the memory bank you build together is so important. The lasting memories one of you will leave for the other is a legacy of love.

Some of the most bittersweet and endearing conversations I've shared with widowed people are about their loved ones. Most of them don't recollect the bad times or the things their mates did that irritated them. They are too busy reminiscing about all the good times they shared--those are the only times that count.

Though their partners are gone, the love and good memories left behind still flourish. It's sad to see these people who can only embrace their memories while they ache to hold their loved ones again. It's also poignant to hear them talk so fondly of the memories they built together and the good qualities their mates possessed. The positive memory banks they built will stay with them forever. Their vivid remembrances give many of them the vitality to live out their remaining years. They take solace in knowing that the love their partners left behind will never leave them.

One reason the blockbuster movie *Ghost* touched many people in such a special way is because many of us would give anything to hold a deceased loved one again and tell them we love them once more. In the romantic thriller, when Molly gets to hold Sam (played by Demi Moore and Patrick Swayze) one last time, there are no dry eyes because we all know how priceless that moment would be.

Don't wait. Make it a point to remember to love now. Don't dwell on what irritates you. Instead, reflect on the memories and good times you build together. Build as many positive memories together as you can.

Remember to focus on the positive qualities your mate possesses. If it means seeing your private little world through rose colored glasses, take them out, dust them off, and dream on. So what if love colors your vision--sometimes love is the best color of all.

Using your Married Mistress Workbook (see page 15), complete the following exercises.

The New Eyes Exercise

List five things your mate does that bother you.

What could you tactfully do to let him know these things irritate you?

Old Eyes Exercise

List five qualities that strongly attracted you to him.

Have any of these qualities changed?

Yes No

If yes, what will it take to rekindle your attraction?

Write a short paragraph explaining why you picked him to share in a lifetime of loving.

List five ways your life would dramatically change if your mate left or died.

List three of your best memories of your life together so far.

Nine

What About You?

Are You Content?

Your happiness is crucial to the well-being of your intimate union. Many experts tout the key to keeping your relationship monogamous is to keep your man happy. I disagree. Your satisfaction and happiness are crucial to your relationship. If you get what you want and need out of the relationship, you will be willing to give more. A healthy spousal relationship entails both parties receiving mutual satisfaction. Self-interest is one of the most important qualities a married mistress can possess. *If you are not content, your union will definitely suffer.*

Being a married mistress doesn't include a woman doing everything to please her mate at her expense. If she does and he fails to consider her needs, their liaison will eventually suffer because she will tire of carrying the one-way responsibility. The marital affair is a *two-way street*. The result promises mutual gratification.

Secret:

> The other woman usually makes sure the man she's involved with plays an active role in their affair.

For women who think most men won't work at a relationship, let's go back to the extramarital affair for a moment. The other woman can't have an affair alone. It takes two people to (shall we say) tangle.

The married man involved in this cloak of secrecy must make a number of arrangements to see his other woman. If he meets her in a hotel room, he must rent the room, reserve time to sneak away to meet her, lie to his wife, shower, shave, and drown himself in sexy cologne--all to meet her. Then, on top of all that, he has to cover his tracks! If a married man can put this much effort into a forbidden affair, he can put the same kind of energy into a marital affair. *And he will--if he wants the relationship badly enough.*

When a married man is with his mistress, they leave the world outside for whatever time they have together. They make sure they both benefit from their liaison. The marital affair follows the same idea. It has to be something both of you want and *are willing to do what it takes to make it work.*

One of Her Most Potent Secrets:

> The other woman does not lose sight of her needs to fulfill her married lover's needs.

How many mistresses do you see foregoing their wants to please their men? One mistress has been dating her sister's husband for over a year. She explains why she feels her needs are important to their relationship. "When Jay and I are together, he likes to see me happy. He knows I value my well-being. I take care of myself. My sister Sue is different because all she ever talks about is what the kids need and what Jay needs. Then she complains about how she never gets anything. She acts like she's not partly to blame. Jay says he respects me because I don't lose myself in our relationship. I'm my own woman. I'll never see my whole identity as just someone's wife or mother."

Many of the mistresses interviewed for this book believe in doing what it takes to make themselves happy. Wives can learn a powerful lesson from the other woman's self-interest.

One wife quoted in a *Woman's World Magazine* article about lasting marriages already knows the importance of taking care of self. "If your kids and your husband are your whole life, you're headed for trouble," says Marie. "When you are lonely or upset, you'll blame them." Marie, who has enjoyed a blissfully happy marriage for many years, says her marriage to her husband, Joe, is the biggest but not the *only* source of joy in her life.

Your Needs Are Important

Have you asked yourself what you want from your marital affair? If not, determine what you want more of from your mate. Make sure he does not overlook your needs. On a scale of one to ten (ten being the best) you are probably a nine or ten as a partner and mother. But how do you rate as a woman who values her own needs? In a later chapter, I'll be discussing ways you can treat yourself special. But for now it's important to remember that being a married mistress is not just about pleasing him; it's also about pleasing you.

Knowing Who Your Friends Are

It's a disappointing reality that when a man becomes involved in an adulterous affair, sometimes his partner in crime is his wife's best friend or, like Jay's mistress, a close family member. That gives the wife a distressing double blow to confront. Many mistresses interviewed for this book knew the wife in their triangle intimately. I talked to sisters, best friends, and other close friends of the woman they were betraying. It's an unpleasant situation, but one that needs discussing. Knowing who your friends are and what to divulge to your closest girlfriend is the subject of the next chapter.

Please answer the following questions in your Married Mistress Workbook (see page 15).

Needs Assessment Exercise

◆ Are you 100% satisfied with your intimate relationship?

◆ What can your man do to help improve it?

◆ Are you accustomed to telling him when you feel he is not meeting your needs?

◆ On a scale of one to ten, (ten being the best) rate yourself as:
> Wife
> Co-worker
> Mother
> A woman who takes care of her needs

◆ Make a wish list of what you want from your mate in your intimate relationship.

Ten

Best Friends and Lovers

It's a double-edged sword. The ultimate betrayal. One of the most hurtful experiences a woman can endure is discovering that her man is sleeping with her best friend. You trust both of them with your life, and they are responsible for destroying it.

"When I found out my husband was sleeping with my best friend it felt like someone stuck a knife in my heart and kept twisting it over and over," Mona painfully remembers. Her sixteen year marriage is on the verge of crumbling upon Mona's discovery that her husband has been having an affair with her best friend for over eight years. "I felt like life dealt me a double-whammy. She was my best friend! How could they do that to me?"

Why would any woman commit such an unforgivable violation, piercing the heart of a friend she supposedly loves? Barb, the woman who has been sleeping with her best friend's husband, John, for over eight years, summed it up when she admitted that as the other woman: *"You become numb to the guilt."* That's a powerful statement. Many wives think their best friend will never cross that uncrossable boundary, and many will not. Nevertheless, everyday in this country men cheat on their wives, and, all too often, their partners in lust are close friends or family members.

Usually, the best friend doesn't deliberately set out to destroy the marriage. Barb says she didn't. Mona and Barb had been the closest of friends for over twenty years. After her husband left her, Barb moved in with Mona and John to try and pick up the pieces of her life. Mona took Barb in and shared everything with her. She and her husband no longer did things as a couple. Mona, John, and Barb became a threesome.

Mona talked to Barb about everything. She revealed her most intimate secrets to Barb, including her and John's love life. Barb thought things were great between Mona and her mate, but Mona revealed private thoughts and trouble on the horizon. Meanwhile, John began confiding in Barb about his wife's lack of interest in him and sex. At first, Barb, trying to be a good friend, offered advice and tried to bring the two people she loved most in this world together as a couple. However, as John confided in her more and more, she began to feel strangely attracted to her friend's husband.

Mona, growing weary of the lack of closeness between them, began withdrawing from her husband even further, encouraging him to spend more time with Barb. After all, Barb had just gone through an ugly break up with her husband. She needed both of them to be there for her.

And John was there--more and more. He began experiencing the same feelings of forbidden attraction to Barb. They fought off their feelings, but after months of being together in the same house while other interests occupied Mona's time, they succumbed to their bodily passions. The sexual undercurrents shared between them finally pulled them under.

Barb felt extremely guilty at first, feeling as if she had taken advantage of Mona's kindness and friendship. But the more time passed and she realized she truly loved John, the easier it became to block out her remorse. As Barb admitted, after awhile, she simply didn't feel guilty. After eight years, Mona found out John was sleeping with her best friend. Ironically, when she began suspecting he was cheating on her, Barb is the one Mona confided in about her suspicions. It didn't even cross her mind that Barb was the other woman in John's life.

Barb moved out of her best friend's house and now rents an apartment across town. John meets her in the apartment as often as he can. She says they plan to marry soon; John is going to ask Mona for a divorce. Mona has come face-to-face with the brutal shock of her husband's adulterous crime with her closest friend.

We All Make Mistakes

Barb, John, and Mona all made major mistakes. Barb crossed into dangerous territory. When she sensed her feelings for John growing into something more than friendship, her first instinct was to remove herself from the situation. Now she will constantly have to ask herself if what she gained with John was worth risking her lifelong friendship with Mona.

John made the classic mistake many men who commit adultery make. Instead of communicating his frustrations to his wife when he sensed his marriage was in trouble, he confided in her best friend. That automatically created a dangerous bond between them. If he had talked to his wife when he felt she was losing interest in him, he may have avoided his dangerous liaison with Barb. Many men admit that they have a difficult time confronting their partners about intimate issues. They prefer to delay arguments and avoid creating bad feelings. But what kind of emotions did John think he would face when Mona found out about his infidelity? Not only does he have to deal with Mona's feelings of anger and betrayal, he must also contend with the pain he has caused his teenage children. He would have dealt with a lot less pain and anguish if he had talked to Mona the moment they began having problems. Instead, he took the path that initially caused less friction. But, his route ended up causing everyone involved and others around them a lot of unnecessary grief.

And what about Mona? What part did she play in this? Though Mona did not commit the crime, the two-fold part she played in it was significant. She made her first mistake when she turned a deaf ear to her troubled relationship with John. Her second equally damaging error in judgement was confiding in her best friend. That's what friends are for, you may say. While it's true your best friend is the one you usually confide in, certain details are better left unsaid, *even to a best girlfriend.*

"Girlfriend, Let Me Tell You"

You want to share everything with your best friend. Your hopes, dreams, fears, and your happiness. *Nevertheless, sharing private moments enjoyed between husband and wife crosses a taboo.*

Another secret:

> Telling the other woman about the intricacies of y o u r   i n t i m a t e relationship is like giving her a loaded gun to aim directly at your face.

Whether she uses the ammunition you supplied her with to turn your life into a living hell is entirely up to her. Mona didn't realize she was confiding in the other woman. She thought she was sharing intimate information with her best friend. But anyone can become the other woman. You never know when you are in the company of a woman who would sleep with your husband. And you can't control another person's actions. You can, however, follow certain guidelines to keep from helping the other woman. One of these rules to adhere to stringently is *keep the private details of your marriage between you and your mate.*

Your Best Friend

There is another important rule you can live by. Your best friend, the person you can share every secret detail of your soul and trust with your innermost thoughts--*is your mate.* He is your best friend. In a study conducted for her book, *The Successful Woman,* Dr. Joyce Brothers asked couples what was most important in sustaining a long, loving relationship. Her findings discounted the myth that sex is most important in an intimate relationship. Dr. Brothers found that while sex ranked twelfth in importance to men, it came in fourteen for women. What did rank number one for both sexes, however, was:

♦ *"That their spouse was their best friend."*

By trusting each other with intimate details and sharing your thoughts and emotions with each other, you're doing more than being good partners. You're becoming best friends.

Part II
Communication:
The Strongest Link

Eleven

Are You Listening to Me?

The Communication Link

The communication link is the one link that keeps all the others firmly in place--it's the strongest link in your marital chain. Without it, your union will suffocate. Communication encompasses every facet of your intimate union; it's what gives your relationship the solid ground to stand on. The results of a study conducted at Wayne University revealed that the best single predictor of overall marital satisfaction is a couple's ability to use communication to solve problems when they arise.

Manspeak Versus Womanspeak

Since communication is such an integral part of your spousal relationship, understanding one another's way of verbalizing is a boundary many couples must cross to improve their communication skills.

If you didn't know it already, men and women speak in different tongues. Most of the time the language of the male gender, known as Manspeak, consists of little more than a few inaudible grunts here and there, a confusing sports lingo closely resembling lawyer jargon, and a lot of mechanical "yes, dears." Men created the "yes, dear" phrase to pacify women and keep them off their backs so they could continue sharing grunts between the sports jargon vital to the male bonding process.

I may be a little biased, but the language of women, called Womanspeak, is more advanced. Punctuated with emotion, it is often more inquisitive (men may call it nosy) than Manspeak (and it calls for many times the volume of words used in Manspeak).

A humorist joked that one reason women and men don't communicate well is because men speak about 15,000 words a day while women, on average, speak 25,000 to 30,000 words a day. That means when he comes home after a long day's work, his 15,000 utterances are exhausted. You, on the other hand, having spoken about 15,000 words, are just getting your second wind!

It doesn't take a person with Einstein's I.Q. to figure out that men and women communicate differently. But knowing that, what can we do about it? How can you get him to open up and say what's on his mind? How can you get your message across without him tagging it as nagging? How can you better understand one another?

A Common Language

The goal is understanding each other without changing your individual self-expression. You don't want to change your way of conversing, and you don't want him to totally change his. (Do you?) One of the most celebrated factors about men and women is that we are different. It's this interesting mixture of contrasts that add the spice and excitement in your intimate relationship. Removing too much of the spice ruins the recipe. However, you do want to come to a common ground with your mate and create a mutual understanding. There is a practical path to reaching that commonality. This direct route calls for:

> *Mutual*
> *Respect*

By respecting each other's differences you are, in effect, saying you understand one another. That acknowledgement means understanding that *each* of you brings a uniqueness to the relationship and can respect the differences. That understanding will bring you to a common ground.

The Art of Effective Communication

Most people think speaking eloquently equals good communication, but talking is only part of getting your message across. An equally significant part often overlooked is attentive listening. "It irritates me when I'm talking to my husband, and he's just waiting for me to pause so he can run away with the conversation. Most of the time, he hasn't heard a word I've said." Many men and women I interviewed cloned Sharon's comments. Many said they have a spouse who does not know how to listen.

Fine Tuning Your Listening Skills

Good listening skills are not innate. Active listening is a skill best developed with practice and concentrated effort. Mortimer J. Adler, author of *How To Speak/How To Listen* says it amazes him that people generally assume that the ability to listen well is a "natural gift" requiring no skill. He also emphasizes that listening is an "untaught skill" and says there is no effort made in our entire educational system to help individuals learn how to listen.

Passive listening occurs when an individual isn't making an effort to hear and understand what the other person says. Typically, when someone listens passively, their preoccupation with another activity robs their attention. They could be thinking about something going on in their life, a task needing completion, or simply waiting to get the next word in.

Active listening calls for a clear mind. This is the only type of effectual listening. The best way to become an active listener is with practice. When you and your partner take an active role in listening to each other, you strengthen your intimate relationship, and each of you will know that when you are talking about something important to you, your words will not fall on deaf ears.

Getting Attention

It's essential when you talk to your partner, you make sure you have his attention. This is where mutual respect plays into the picture again. If something else has his attention, or it's evident he's not in a listening mode, it's best to wait and approach him at another time. If you cannot wait, you must say something to get his attention. Effective communication calls for being direct. If there's another activity stealing his attention, ask him if he can put it aside for a moment because you have something important to say.

There's nothing wrong with making sure the other person is listening. If you see signs of wandering, simply ask, "Honey, are you listening to me?" This serves two purposes. First, it helps your mate refocus his attention. Second, it gives you the peace of mind of knowing you have recaptured his attention. Thus, when you continue, you know he's not passively listening.

Helping each other learn to become better listeners takes time, patience, and a good deal of practice. Don't expect results overnight. If one or both of you are in the habit of passive listening, active listening will take time to learn. Be patient and reward each other for progress by giving praise that says, "I'm glad you're such a good listener."

The Closed Man

What if you want to fine tune your listening skills, but your man won't give you much to listen to? According to Ryan Vollmer in his magazine article, "Silent Partner," having a closed man surfaced as one of the most irritating things for women to struggle with. Many men close themselves off to certain subjects. One of those high on their closed list is intimate details. Women are usually more adept communicators than men when the subject involves intimacy. Early on, women are programmed to be more in tune with their emotions than men because women are given carte blanche to display emotion:

At age four, Jane scrapes her knee. She cries and her mother immediately consoles her. Johnny, also four, receives the same encouragement to absolve his pain with tears.

At fifteen, Jane cries because she got passed over for the cheerleading squad. Again, her parents comfort her and encourage Jane to communicate her disappointment with tears. When the football coach passes fifteen-year-old Johnny up for the varsity football team and Johnny allows a tear slip down his face, his father immediately chastises him. Johnny's father reminds him, as he has ever since Johnny was five or six, that men don't cry. That means men bottle-up their emotions and keep them hidden. That's what real men do.

We meet Jane again at age thirty-five. This time her supervisor passed her over for a well-deserved promotion. She bursts into the house in tears. This time her husband lends the compassionate shoulder encouraging her to let it out. John's boss passed him over for a promotion for the fifth time in as many years, but thirty-five-year-old John doesn't come home to seek the understanding arms of his wife. Instead, he drowns his anguish in a few cold, stiff beers at his local pub. When he does go home, he's so intoxicated, all he does is fall into bed. He avoids letting his wife share in his pain because he believes real men don't feel pain.

As Dr. Herb Goldberg, author of *The Hazards Of Being Male* puts it, "The echoes of 'Big boys don't cry,' and 'Crybaby!'" resonate deep within the male psyche and block the flow of tears and the full experience of sadness." Women can play a vital role in helping men break down those old stereotypes.

Trust

Are you ready for your man to show his emotions? Don't take that question too lightly. You have to make sure he can trust you with his protected emotional vault he's locked away since childhood. If he opens up and you aren't ready for it, you'll put up a brick wall so massive it will never topple. In an earlier chapter, Stanley, who left his wife for his mistress, admitted that one reason behind the move was after his wife, Alice, encouraged him to show his emotions, she ridiculed him for being weak.

The Nice Guy Trap

In the revealing book, *Why Can't Men Open Up?* writers Steven Naifeh and Gregory White Smith say that while most women say they want men to be more loving and intimate, many times, they can't handle a show of raw emotion from their man. "Most women insist that they want men who express vulnerability, shed tears, and show affection." But the authors contend that while the closed man frustrates most women, he also fascinates them. "He is both the unresponsive, inaccessible man who refuses to share his feelings or give emotional support *and* the shadowy romantic male who lurks in many women's fantasies." They go on to say that women want men to be vulnerable but invincible. Smith shares his somber story about how he received accolades from his father when he hid his emotions, but he wonders where the praise is for his pent-up emotions now that he is a grown man who has yet to shed a single tear for his brother who died over a decade ago. Like most men, he deals with his gut-wrenching pain in silence.

Smith is typical of most men in that he wants to learn how to express intimate emotions. For these men, their women can hold the key to teaching them how to open up by allowing them to express their feelings. If your man senses that you cannot handle his vulnerabilities, he will not open up to you. He has to know he can trust you with his emotions. Remember, when society taught him that men don't cry, it was a message you also learned. Your thinking may also require reprogramming.

Building Bridges

Psychologist Sidney Cohen, author of the article, "A Common Language," has a very productive suggestion for couples who find themselves in the heat of repeated fruitless arguments. He suggests couples consider coming up with their own *"couple's dictionary."* For example, financial security may mean one thing to you and something altogether different to your mate. By clearly defining different issues, both of you will understand and learn to respect one another's differences.

Effective communication is a learned skilled. We aren't born knowing how to communicate. Couples who take the time to listen to each other and actively keep the lines of communication open strengthen their intimate relationships. They know how to use communication to build bridges, not tear them down.

Twelve

Constructive Confrontation

Sarah gets off work at five and realizes she only has thirty minutes to make it to the local gas station before it closes. She races to her car and speeds off, trying to beat the clock. Just before pulling up to the pump, a guy in a white Chevy pick-up rudely cuts her off. "That's O.K.," she says to herself. She reasons that he's probably in a hurry, too, so she lets her temporary irritation roll off her back and patiently waits her turn. After she gets the gas and walks towards the store, another patron bumps into Sarah, crunching her right foot under one of his steel-toe army boots. He wasn't watching where he was going because he was too busy ogling the redhead at the gas pump. He manages to tear his eyes away to mumble, "Sorry ma'am."

"Oh, no problem," she weakly gasps while wiggling her toes to make sure he did not break any of them. She hobbles into the convenience mart to pay the cashier.

"What pump are you on?" The store clerk rudely inquires while crossing his arms, impatiently waiting for Sarah's hesitant reply. She humbly admits that she didn't notice the number on the pump. The clerk throws up his hands in disgust and sarcastically spits out, "Oh, that's just great!"

"What a rude person," Sarah says silently, not daring to speak out. Being discourteous to a stranger would be rude. Sarah pays him and limps back to her car so she can rush home and soak her sore foot. On the way, a police officer pulls her over for picking up speed through a yellow light. Something in the back of her mind says this is not her night. He is offensively rude to Sarah, making a lewd comment about "women drivers," but after he hands her the ticket she automatically *thanks* him. "We're supposed to thank mannerless cops who give us tickets," she rationalizes.

Sarah finally makes it home. Luckily, it's her husband's turn to cook, and he already has dinner on the table. She sits down at the dining room table still absorbing the enormous pain in her right foot and still annoyed about the clerk's attitude and that ticket she didn't think she deserved.

"Honey," Sarah's husband lovingly calls to her, "can you please pass me the salt?" That does it. She explodes. She glares at her husband, nostrils flaring while angrily hurling insults his way. *"I just can't do enough for you--can I! I guess you'll be demanding the pepper next!"* With that, Sarah jumps out of her chair and indignantly limps into the bedroom, too enraged to finish dinner. A bit of guilt creeps into Sarah's thoughts. She realizes that her unwarranted outburst at her husband will cause friction between them but, once again, she reasons to herself, *"I just had to tell somebody off."*

Many times, like Sarah, we avoid confronting people we don't know, acting as if we can't show outsiders our bad side. Unfortunately, we save that side for people who know and love us, our husband, our children, our family. They are all too often allowed the privilege of our misguided wrath. One married mistress said she believes the reason we do that is because we know what to expect from our loved ones. They offer us a safe outlet. On the other hand, challenging a stranger means exploring unknown territory--for many of us, that can be intimidating.

Dr. Wayne W. Dyer, author of *Pulling Your Own Strings,* confirms that fear often paralyzes people. He says that when a person is in a threatening situation with a stranger, a question that may come to mind is "what will happen if..."

When the clerk was rude to Sarah, her fear of his unknown reaction led her to ask herself, "What if he gets angry with me if I say he's discourteous?" Her fear of the police officer was even more significant--"What if he raises my fine, or what if he hauls me off to jail?"

Unresolved Conflicts

Clearly, fear of the unknown often coerces some people to bite their tongues in the presence of strangers. However, what often happens when we have an unpleasant experience with a stranger or co-worker that leaves us feeling hurt or angry, is these feelings go unresolved. When that occurs, it is not uncommon for us to "should" on ourselves:

- I should have said
- I should have done
- I shouldn't have gone

We frequently try to satisfy "should haves" through someone else. We allow the controversy to brew in our minds until, sometimes, we end up trying to resolve the conflict or, at least, obtain temporary satisfaction by blowing off steam at an innocent bystander.

Sarah was right to speak out about her discontent--keeping it bottled up causes anxiety. Her common error, however, was trying to vindicate her anger by directing it toward the wrong person. If she remains in the habit of venting frustrations caused by the outside world through her husband, their intimate relationship will endure unnecessary conflict. Learning to resolve more outside conflicts helps couples enjoy a more harmonious life.

Speak Up

One way Dr. Dyer suggests finding the courage to face up to unpleasant situations is to ask, "What is the worst thing that could happen to me if...?"

Though Sarah's mishaps that evening were many, she blamed her irritation mainly on the rude store clerk and police officer. By asking herself, "What is the worst thing that could happen to me if I stand up to the clerk or officer," she probably could have worked up the courage to let both the clerk and police officer know, in a calm fashion, that their rudeness was unnecessary. If they continued being brusque, a letter to the police department describing the incident, and a mention to the store manager that she will not be patronizing the gas station because of the discourteous clerk should result in swift action. By doing her part to make sure she verbalizes her views, she will feel empowered because she attempted to resolve the situation.

I encountered an impolite store manager one day when I called up a lingerie store asking for information. While the store clerk was pleasant, the store manager was extremely rude. I calmly got her name and told her I did not appreciate her attitude. She was still discourteous. After I finished talking to her, I called the main office of the store chain and obtained the name of the president and the head of the complaint department.

I immediately wrote a letter explaining why I would not be visiting their store with my hard-earned dollars and sent a copy of the letter to three people: the president of the chain, the head of the complaint department, and the rude store manager. Within days, I received a formal apology in the form of a personal phone call from the head of the complaint department. Even if I had not received acknowledgement of the letter, I felt I resolved the situation just by writing it. And instead of being angry or saying "I should have" when I went home, I shared what happened with my husband and told him how I resolved the situation to my satisfaction.

Don't be afraid to speak up when you feel people are treating you unfairly. In the case of employees who work with the public, the majority of them are courteous and helpful. But the handful of sour seeds need to realize that rudeness is not part of their job description. Public service associations and stores would not be in business long if the public did not patronize them. A customer should never be an irritant; they are the reason that establishment stays in business.

We All Have Our Days

The paper shredder accidentally gobbles up your thirty page document. Your tire went flat. The cleaners closed before you picked up your business suit you planned to wear to your important annual meeting. The day care center called you to pick up your daughter, who won't stop crying. Things are not going well. When life's irritations get the best of us, it's not difficult to come home with pent-up frustration. When that happens to you or your spouse, the situation calls for honesty. A pleasant, "Honey, I've had a bad day," or "I have a splitting headache," goes a long way in letting your partner know you need space and time to regroup. There will be times when you become your spouse's venting bag. When that happens, acknowledge his anger and calmly let him know that you understand, but you are not the source of his problem.

Times will crop up, however, when your partner *is* at the root of your frustration. In this case, the person you need to constructively confront is him. The next chapter discusses things you should say and definite no-no's when arguing with your mate.

Thirteen

"I Hate You, You Jerk!"

Sticks and Stones

Toxic words hurt. Like poison, they can unwittingly seep into the situation, disintegrating the road to sound trust and communication with your love partner. One man admitted that his escape from his wife's sharp criticism and vicious verbal attacks is his mistress. "My wife, Susan, can be downright cruel. When she gets on a roll, she calls me every name in the book, and some that aren't even in there. We argue constantly. When I've had enough, I go to see Shawna, my girlfriend. She rebuilds my ego after Susan tears it down."

Secret:

> Constant bickering and angry words exchanged between you and your spouse spells trouble for you, but can mean an open door for the other woman.

Couples in healthy intimate relationships don't use arguments for the sole purpose of hurting each other's feelings, attests Scott Winoker in his magazine article, "What Happy Couples Do Right." On the other hand, Winoker affirms that unhappy couples practice lashing out at each other, calling names, or showing contempt for the other's point of view. These types of showdowns are dangerous to the health of any intimate connection. Sticks and stones can break bones, but words break hearts. And unlike bones, broken hearts don't mend as easily.

When I'm conducting a seminar, I almost always have one person in the class exclaim that they have never experienced an argument with their spouse in their umpteen years of marriage. That kind of statement makes me nervous. In the book, *Husbands And Wives,* Dr. Melvyn Kinder and Dr. Connell Cowan attest that most arguing is really "an intense form of impassioned communication." They also say that couples who experience the desire to avoid fights and shy away from disagreements are often the ones whose marriages can be in more danger because they hide behind what they call "a veil of congeniality and seeming harmony." Avoiding arguments is not the answer--healthy couples argue, they just know how to fight fair.

Positive Arguing

Couples engage in basically two types of arguing: *Positive arguing* and *negative arguing.* Positive arguing is a productive form of reasoning. The purpose? To solve problems, listen to one another, and build strong lines of communication.

Negative arguing, the type unhappy couples employ the most, is more like a cat fight. Negative arguing calls for each participant to remove the boxing gloves and begin hissing and scratching his or her opponents eyes out. The purpose? To tear each other and the relationship apart. Dr. Judith Sills says when we feel rage, we often aim it right at the heart of our loved ones. In her magazine article, "When You Hate The One You Love," she acknowledges that uncontrollable rage can play an unhealthy role in arguing. Unfortunately, rage often reigns supreme in couples who argue negatively.

Positive arguing is such an important facet in an intimate relationship that many major universities now teach couples the art. In her magazine article titled "Men VS Women," Patricia Volk stresses that like sex, "fighting is a form of communication. You have to know how to love. And you have to know how to fight."

Positive arguing basically requires six major elements:

- Skill
- Tact
- Patience

- Practice
- Compromise
- Humor

Skill

To fight fair, you and your mate must become gracefully adept at dodging what I call destructive urges. In the heat of passionate anger, it's not unusual to feel like you want to lash out or strike back in defense of a criticism. When your partner says or does something that makes you angry, take a quick breather and think before you speak. This is possible in an angry moment, but it requires skill. It takes practice re-learning how to react to a volatile situation.

When we were children, others sometimes unwittingly taught us poor debating skills. Many of us learned from watching parents, siblings, or other adults. The best way to break out of this cycle is to refocus your energies on practicing skillful or thoughtful confrontation instead of worrying about a counter-attack.

Tact

It's difficult to be tactful when you're angry, but positive arguing calls for tact. One of the easiest ways you and your partner can learn to use tact in your arguments is to practice taking responsibility for your feelings. "I feel" is a phrase that adds tact to a potentially explosive situation. When you accuse your mate by saying things like,

> "Why did you use this?"
> "Can't you do anything right?"
> "Why did you need this anyway?"

Those kinds of statements automatically put him on the defensive. However, if you change these statements to:

> "I feel hurt when you use this without asking."
> "I feel a little upset when you leave without telling me."
> "I feel left out when you don't tell me about your purchases."

Instead of placing blame, you are taking responsibility for how the situation makes you feel. By doing this, you remove the defensive atmosphere, and your mate will not feel as if he needs to vindicate himself. By using tact, both of you can learn to discuss the situation rationally.

Patience

Both of you must learn to be patient with each other while re-learning positive arguing tactics. You also need to be patient with yourself. If you've been practicing negative arguing skills, re-learning new ones won't be easy nor will the skill come quickly. Positive arguing takes patience. The rewards may be slow in coming, but the results are well worth it.

Practice

Developing good debating skills takes practice, practice, and more practice. Think of each bout with your partner as a practice session. Don't purposely revive a dead issue to practice your fighting skills, but do utilize each opportunity to polish your positive arguing techniques. And if either of you slip back into old habits, use one of the most under utilized words in the dictionary: *Sorry (make sure it's sincere)*. A heartfelt apology helps build goodwill. By using each disagreement to encourage both of you to remove harmful land mines out of your intimate battlefield, you'll both soon become winners in the art of communication.

Compromise

Dr. Judith Sills says that whenever you need to be in the winner's circle every time a confrontation occurs, what you usually win instead of love is a constant struggle for power. In her magazine article, "Getting Your Own Way," Sills maintains that control is seductive. "Compromise is not nearly as gratifying as out-and-out victory, and that makes it easy to forget that your triumph represents someone else's defeat."

"Compromise is essential in positive confrontation. Negotiating an agreement, rather than holding to one-sided expectations, is an important tool to get more of what you want in your relationship," according to Ellen Sue Stern, in her magazine article, "Too Many Expectations." Negotiation is especially essential because of most men's emotional makeup.

Ask the majority of men and they will concede that they do not like to argue with their partners. Many more of them give in to their spouses so they can avoid confronting the issue at hand. A husband will usually let his wife decorate the house the way she wants, dress up the yard to her liking, let her decide what clothes to buy for the children (some take it as far as allowing their wives to pick *their* clothes), and give in on doing household chores her way.

With all this one-sided compromise going on, don't think that because a man gives in he is content. He usually feels frustrated and feels he has little say about what goes on in his own household. But, as I said earlier, most men usually won't challenge their wives. What many of them will do is much more threatening to the marriage; they often use this excuse to turn to the arms of another woman.

Another secret:

> Especially in the beginning of the majority of most extramarital relationships, the man enjoys a lot of control.

He lets his other woman know when he can get away to see her. He leaves when he has to. He secretly calls her when he can sneak away from his wife. He is in control. A man who exercises little authority in his home environment can easily become intoxicated by his newfound power. One man says he welcomes his commanding role in his extramarital relationship. "At home, Lois is the boss, plain and simple. She clumps me along with the dog, and kids, telling us all what to eat, how to act, and so on. With Marge, I come and go as I please. Basically, I'm calling all the shots."

Compromise with your spouse. Learn to give in now and then and encourage his opinion. After all, your ultimate goal is to live together in a harmonious environment. The only way that can happen is for both of you to be content.

Humor

Doctors Kinder and Cowan affirm that humor serves as a very effective tool in diffusing a heated battle. It's hard to be angry when you're laughing. Susie, a married mistress, tells how her boyfriend sometimes turns their arguments around with his unique brand of humor. "Sometimes Dan and I will be in the most heated argument, says Susie, with a wide grin, "I'll be pointing my finger and getting really intense and then, all of the sudden, Dan will get this mischievous look on his face, then he'll run over, pick me up, and run around the house with me draped across one shoulder. By the time he lets me down, we're both cracking up laughing. Who can stay mad?"

Chris, another married mistress, puts an interesting twist on her humor skills to diffuse her passionate arguments with her beau. "My mom told me whenever someone is chewing me out, picture them in their underwear so I can maintain my sense of humor. I use this technique with Jim from time to time, but it's not because picturing *him* in his underwear makes me laugh. No--when I picture my sexy man that way, I don't laugh, but I can bet you one thing--the heated argument ends pretty quickly. We usually end up moving our conversation into the bedroom--then we move directly into the making up stage. By the way, Jim also uses this technique on me--it works every time."

Whatever unique skills you and your beau acquire, the ultimate goal of fighting is to break destructive patterns. By using positive arguing skills and thinking of each confrontation as a way of building up your skills, you strengthen your intimate relationship.

The next chapter discusses two more important elements in communicating with your mate: praise and criticism.

Fourteen

A Pat on the Back Doesn't Hurt

A sentiment echoed by many men who stray is that the other woman makes them feel good about themselves.

Secret:

> Most men who date the other woman agree that she knows how to stroke a man's ego.

One man who met his paramour of two years on the job had this to say: "Marsha lets me know how magnificent I am in bed or tells me how sexy I look. She even notices if I'm wearing a new tie. I could leave for work in the morning with a butcher knife covered with blood in one hand and a severed head in the other, and my wife wouldn't even notice. Some mornings she doesn't even know I've left for work. Marsha is always happy to see me and sad when I leave. And when I do leave, she makes sure I'll want to come back. Things used to be that way with my wife but that was years ago."

This man's wife is unaware that she is an accomplice in his extramarital affair. Her husband said he repeatedly tried to communicate the need for his wife to notice him and make him feel good about himself. They even sought counseling at one point in their marriage. He claimed having the affair was a last resort. He also admitted that his need for praise was a driving force in this decision.

Praise makes us feel good. Remember how you beamed when you were a child and you brought home a good report card? The only thing more gratifying than your success was your parents' acknowledgement of it. That same child who grinned from ear to ear whenever receiving praise still lives inside the heart of most adults. It's not uncommon for your man to seek praise. Where he finds it is up to you.

Why Should I Praise Him?

It's not up to you to do all the praising. If one person in a relationship gives all the applause and the other person fails to reciprocate, pretty soon all praise will stop because the one person giving it will tire. Think a moment about the extramarital affair. If you think that the men who have long-term mistresses are receiving all the accolades and not giving any back, think again. Not only do these men verbalize how wonderful their mistresses are, they show them in other ways. Showering the other woman with gifts, inundating her with flowers, and whisking her away to romantic places. By learning a lesson in praise from her, all the attention she receives can be yours (and rightfully so). Also, when you hold your man in high esteem and uplift his spirits, you teach him to do the same for you. Often, men learn how to treat women better from the example they get from a woman who knows how to treat a man.

A Word About Criticism

"Don't." That succinct advice comes from Bob Berkowitz, author of the tell all book, *What Men Won't Tell You But Women Need To Know*. He maintains that most men do not relish criticism. Taking that a step further, neither do women. None of us enjoys hearing someone tell us what's wrong with us. Television ads bombard us all day telling us our breath stinks, our job is lousy, our car is second-class at best, and our body odor is rancid. Next, supervisors fill out critique sheets (not praise sheets, mind you) on job performance telling us what we've been doing wrong this quarter. The last thing most of us need is a loved one dumping more criticism in our laps.

Doctors Kinder and Cowan say that you experience a sense of satisfaction when you conquer the impulse to "ram the 'truth' down someone's throat." In her book about criticism, Dr. Deborah Bright maintains that criticism is inherently negative, and it can be very hurtful. She says almost everyone has a "host of uncomfortable associations related to criticism in one form or another, and most of us want to avoid receiving too much of it."

Still, what about when your spouse is doing something that

annoys you? Avoiding the situation won't work. Sometimes criticism must come into play, but doled out in small doses and sweetened with praise, it is easier to take. Making it a point to look for the good intertwined with what you conceive as bad or undesirable will soften the critical blow. When you serve criticism in small doses, you make it much more acceptable.

Praise the Boy

Sometimes it's easier for us to praise our small son than it is our spouse. That's because society teaches men, as well as women, that men don't need it. When we see our little boys displaying raw emotion, we know they need praise from us. However, when boys grow up they learn to put on that tough armor called Manhood, shielding themselves from any hint of neediness. But you know what? There is still a two-year-old boy inside that manly man, yearning to get his pat on the back. Remember that the next time you see someone praising a young boy. Joanne remembers praising a co-worker's five-year-old son. "When he introduced his son I was telling the little tyke how handsome he was. He was beaming, and his eyes were just shining. Then I told him what a big boy he was and went on to praise him. Well, when I looked up, his dad was red as a tomato from his balding head to his neck! He was blushing as if he had received all that praise. The little boy inside my co-worker beamed with pride about the cute little life he had a hand in creating. I tested your theory without even realizing it." Though most men may not show it by outwardly blushing as Joanne's co-worker did, they have the same pride-filled reaction because the child inside the man has never left. He's still there hungering to feel good about himself.

Don't Forget the Little Things

How often do you appreciate the good job your mate does keeping the cars in running order? What about taking out the garbage? I know I took those things for granted for a long time. When my husband went out of town on business for a few weeks, the garbage piled up because I forgot to take it to the curb on Wednesdays. I also experienced car trouble after he left. That may sound nonsensical to those of you who take out your trash or do your own auto work, but it wasn't the chore. It was the issue. Just like forgetting to take the trash out and letting it pile up, we sometimes forget to give praise over time, letting unappreciated feelings accumulate. When that happens, we leave the door open for someone else to dole out the praise.

Think about the woman who neglects to tell her man how good he looks when he leaves for the office. She fails to even notice that new cologne he's wearing. When he shows up at work, Charlotte, the office secretary, makes sure she notices. Because she sees an opening, a weak link in Dan's marital chain. She notices Dan's been down in the dumps lately. She's overheard many of his telephone arguments with his wife. She watches his body language and senses he's lonely. She also realizes his wife is helping her out. Dan's never flirted with Charlotte, but she knows she can change that.

Dan's wife can't do anything about Charlotte flirting with him because she can't control what another woman does. She can, however, make sure she does her part to keep her marriage fresh. She can give Dan the praise he needs. By complimenting him on how good he looks now and then, how important he is to her, and by making sure he knows she appreciates him; she has the power to stop Charlotte dead in her tracks.

Try It--It Works

Before I interviewed Jerry I was sure he cheated on his wife. He just fit the mold. He was good looking, and when women walked by our table in the restaurant, they definitely took a moment to glance his way. Jerry is a forty-year-old public relations executive. His black, curly hair and brown tan compliment his green eyes beautifully. He is what most women define as: Hunk material. Jerry married young, at age twenty-five, but he said in all those years he's never been unfaithful to his wife. Of course my next question was, "Why? I mean Jerry, I have to tell you, every woman in this room is practically melting in your presence. Are you sure no one has ever tempted you?"

"Well, I'm not going to lie and say I don't notice women flirting with me. I know this may sound strange, but I'm not always the most confident guy. Diane makes me feel good about myself and not just because she thinks I look good. I've never thought of myself as handsome, and anyway, I'm more concerned with what's inside. That's where Diane comes in. She sees the good inside of me. Even if I don't. She offers me a sanctuary when times are tough. The business world is dog eat dog. And sure, there are women who have hinted they would like to have an office romance with me, but I don't need that in my life. The guys at work call me a straight-arrow because I don't mess around, but I had my share of women before I met Diane. I played the dating game, where I dated three and four women at a time, but all that lying and sneaking around made me uneasy. It just isn't my thing. When I committed to Diane, it was for life. And she makes sure I know I made the right move when I married her. She is always telling me how lucky she is, but I know I'm the lucky one. I don't want anyone else but Diane. Ever."

Fifteen

Superwoman Doesn't Live Here Anymore

While the Women's Liberation movement was still in its heyday, a sexy commercial surfaced on television extolling the virtues of being a liberated, female sexpot. In it, a hot blonde sporting a business suit and briefcase belts out lyrics to the tune *Bad To The Bone* bragging that she can: Bring home the paycheck, cook like Julia Child, and effervescently make love to her man till dawn. She can do all this because she's a WOOOMAN. A liberated woman who has it all. She also gets stuck doing it all.

That was one of the backlashes of the movement. Gloria Steinem, one of the most famous feminists, put it in real terms when she reminded us that she's an example of a woman who doesn't have it all. Steinem is single and she doesn't have children. She focused her life on the struggle for women's rights. While fighting for an equal place in the work force, the women who have families forgot to ask one simple question: Who's going to look after the home?

It turns out that many women ended up trying to synchronize running the household with laboring in the work force. The ongoing battle for women's rights has taught us a lot. Women soon realized the superwoman of the eighties wasn't going to last long if she continued to do it all. Two income families are beginning to share the workload at home. A woman's "place" is no longer in the kitchen, especially if she works eight hours a day in an office. Even if your full-time job is working at home and raising children, you still need a break from the everyday grind. This chapter discusses the 50/50 relationship. Couples are realizing that splitting the chores results in a more rewarding intimate relationship and comfortable home life.

50/50 is the Key

A study conducted by the Families and Work Institute acknowledges that two-income households usually split the housework 70/30 with the woman doing the lion's share. Men and women are both realizing that this imbalance is not working. The best split is the 50/50 split. With both of you sharing the chores, you can expend 50 percent of your time working (in the home and out) while spending the other 50 percent enjoying yourselves, relaxing, and being together as a family and a couple. Doctors Philip Blumstein and Pepper Swartz found in their studies of working couples that when work demands much or all of a person's energy, the intimate relationship may "too easily become a secondary aspect of the individual's life." They maintain that finding time together as a couple presents a taxing challenge, but adequate couple time is essential to a thriving marital affair.

The superwoman of the eighties believed she could do it all. Work eight hours, come home and put in another four hours, and on top of that, be an eager sex kitten, anxiously waiting for her man to come to bed so he could make her moan in ecstasy because she, of course, could *never* let him forget he's a man. What's wrong with that scenario is that when her man (whose only chore consists of plopping down in front of the television, exercising his remote control finger) comes to bed expecting a passionate love partner, what he usually finds is an exhausted wife who definitely forgot he is a man, because she forgot he's even alive. She has been too busy to remember. All the bed begins to represent to her is *sleep*--and he's not about to interfere with that.

"Sex? Are you kidding me?" laughs one married mistress. She says after working eight or nine hours a day, she races to the day care to pick up the boys. Then she runs around the house like a wild woman, fixing dinner, cleaning up after the kids, doing the dishes, bathing their two sons, and putting them to bed. She says she does all this while her hubby lays on the couch watching the tube. "Sometimes I get so mad at him. It doesn't even occur to him to help out. By the time I finish doing all this work it's around 9:30. I have just enough time to sit down for twenty minutes, get back up, take a shower and fall, and I do mean fall into bed in time to get enough rest so I can start over at six a.m. Brad will usually straggle in the bedroom about 10:30. When he starts grabbing on me, I just want him to leave me alone. I'm just too tired. And he has the nerve to wonder why. To me, all our bed represents is a place to rest. I'm just not interested in bedtime sex after I've been working hard all day long.

Maid or Mate?

At some point in their relationship, Susie stopped being Brad's mate and started working as his maid because she felt compelled to take the full burden of the household squarely on her shoulders. A magazine article by Sue Bowder aptly titled "Let It Go," suggests that many women are in what she calls an "over-responsibility trap." They have a built-in mothering instinct, taking care of everything and everyone. After all, our mothers took care of their households like graceful champions. We expect no less from ourselves. But a few generations ago the majority of women stayed home--running the household was their full-time job. Whoever thought that women could grace the work force and effortlessly run the household in one fell swoop was in error--something had to give.

Typically, as in Susie's case, what gives is the intimate relationship. When Susie went from being Brad's love mate to reacting more like a maid in *their* home, both partners suffered. Here's what Brad had to say about the situation: "Susie's such a good mother. She takes care of the house and kids, and she works very hard. I'd notice how she'd look at me like she wanted me to do something. I just didn't know what. I even tried to help her, but she'd end up shooing me away telling me she'd take care of it because it was her job. I hate to see her work so hard, and I do wish we had more time alone together, but Susie's always too tired."

Interestingly enough, I met Brad before I met Susie. Brad phoned after hearing me discuss the 50/50 relationship during a television talk show. He wanted Susie to stop slaving away in the home and start spending more time with him. He encouraged her to sign up for the seminar, and he was one of the first men to take the Monogamous Male Seminar.

Susie quickly came to grips with not living up to the superwoman myth. Instead of throwing dirty looks at Brad, she came up with a list of chores for him to complete. It helped both of them tremendously. She found him an enthusiastic partner willing to share the load, and all she had to do was ask. Both Brad and Susie got what they wanted. Susie got more leisure time, and Brad got his love partner back. As Susie put it, "Now when Brad comes to bed to jump on my bones, they aren't so tired anymore!"

When the majority of men get married, they want a love partner, not a maid. Oftentimes, when their wives make the transition of trading their romantic, lacy-white wedding gloves in for a pair of rubber cleaning gloves, some men seek romance elsewhere.

Another Secret:

> People engaged in extramarital affairs don't waste time with dirty laundry.

One woman who recently took the Married Mistress Seminar one weekend said that she had almost postponed attending the marital enrichment session so she could fold clothes. She admitted afterward that she made the right choice by postponing her laundry in favor of learning ways to improve her marriage.

How many times does your vision of the other woman find her knee-deep in dirty laundry? Can you picture her postponing her time alone with her married lover so she can iron? Two people swept up in the passion of an extramarital affair don't postpone romantic moments.

A man whose wife is in the maid mind-set repeatedly turns him away so she can tend to her overload of chores. This makes it tempting for another woman to woo him away. He knows she won't postpone their intimate moments for dirty laundry.

Talk "Dirty" to Him

Susie's husband Brad, like many men who have taken the Monogamous Male Seminar, wants a closer intimate union with his partner. That fact makes many of these men open to doing their fair share around the house. One suggestion I propose to women who want their partners to help out is: *Talk "dirty" to him.* Now, calm down. I don't mean sexual talk. I'm talking about real dirt: the kind that accumulates on the stove top, floors, and in the bathroom. The best way to get him to split the load is to ask. Let me also say, I don't like the notion that he can "help" you around the house because it still sounds like it is mainly your responsibility. In families where two people work outside the home, the housework must be both parties' responsibility.

Is He Doing It Right?

Ellen Galinsky, president of the Families and Work Institute calls women the "gatekeepers" of the household. How much a husband does around the house correlates directly to how much his wife is willing to let him do. She contends that many times, since a woman is the boss of the house, it's hard for her to turn over the reins to her husband. A woman who claims she wants help from her mate sabotages her efforts when she repeatedly goes behind him redoing every task he completes. And when you ask her why she redoes his chores the standard answer that crops up is:

> *Because he doesn't do it like I would.*

This is a typical reaction from a woman who wants to keep control of the household, but she can't have it both ways. If women want men to do their fair share, they have to let them.

When your mate does his share, if it:
- ♦ Gets cleaned,
- ♦ frees you up,
- ♦ gets him more involved in doing housework,

what more can you ask for? Requiring he perform the task exactly as you do is unfair. Don't look a "work" horse in the mouth. Yes, we are women. Yes, we have the wonderful mothering instinct. And yes, we probably could run our households with one hand tied behind our backs. But do we want to?

What do you want your mark in life to be? That no one can clean like you, not even your mate? Is that what you want people to remember about you? *No one can make those windows shine like she can, not even her husband.* Somehow, I don't think too many people wish they had cleaned better when they grow old and have time to reflect on their life's accomplishments.

If you truly want him to do his share--let him. Let him stack the dishes in the dishwasher the way he wants. If they don't get clean and he has to redo the load a few times, he'll get it together. You may have to show him something complicated, like how to separate the white clothes from colored before tossing them in the wash, but after he gets the hang of it leave him be! So what if he does the colors first and you always do the opposite, washing the white clothes first? As long as it gets done, it doesn't matter how he accomplishes the task.

Gender Benders

Men are exceptionally adept at washing and waxing the car, fixing broken appliances and, don't forget, they're good at changing light bulbs. On the other hand, women are good cooks, better with children than most men, and are the only ones that can carry off the dish pan hands look, right?

Getting stuck in these rigid gender roles can be harmful to a marital relationship. When couples play into stringent gender rules that don't allow men to do dishes or women to mow the lawn, resentment of having the responsibility for the same task day in and day out can settle in and do harm. A recent study by Patricia Ulbrich at the University of Miami revealed that two-income marriages are stressful for some partners because they allow the norms and values that defined gender relations to direct their relationships. At the opposite end, the strongest unions are the ones where both parties have the ability to bend their male/female roles.

Norm and Jennifer, a happily married couple, both attribute their ability to do what they call "cross-training" to making their marriage work. "He's my partner," Jennifer says fondly while lovingly squeezing Norm's hand. "He cleans the table, does dishes, and looks after our three-year-old son; he's a wonderful mother." Norm is quick to return the praise. "She helped me string the electric wire fence around our house. We crawled under the house and did the plumbing, and we rewired the house together." They say they maintain their house as a team. "Just like we rewired the house together," says Norm, "watching our child and doing the housework requires teamwork."

Madison Avenue is also getting in on the act of the changing traditional household roles. Past commercials typically portrayed the man as a foreigner in his own kitchen. The husband who can't hold a spatula straight cooks breakfast for his bedridden wife who's suffering miserably from a debilitating illness (that is the *only* thing that can get this dutiful wife out of the kitchen). This man, who runs his own company, suddenly transforms into a bumbling idiot who can't find his way to the toaster. His spatula singes with pancake batter stuck to it in one hand as he holds up a miserable shirt with a searing imprint of an iron in the other. When the wife finally recuperates, she goes into a set-back after seeing the tornado of a mess her husband left for her to clean up.

Many commercials you see today show men cooking and cleaning with the grace and briskness of their female counterparts. Not only do they know where the toaster is, they don't even scrape the first layer off the top of the toast anymore because they don't burn it. By not allowing your relationship to fall prey to exacting gender roles, you create more of a partnership than traditional marriage allows for. Partners who play (and work) together stay together.

The Stone Age

Some of you may live with a man who enjoys having someone taking care of him. This type of man is not so anxious to bend those gender roles because he likes things the way they are. There are men who quickly settle into having a superwoman around the house. Getting them to do their share may be a little difficult. After all, if you've been cleaning up behind your spouse for a long time, it will be quite a change for him to adjust to his new responsibilities.

Look at it this way. If someone showed up at your house and told you they would cook for you, pick up behind you, and you didn't have to pay them a dime, wouldn't you be a little tempted to take them up on that offer? (After checking their references and confirming they weren't out of their mind, of course.) Well that's where your husband's mentality is. He likes the role you've been playing. It may be difficult at first, but be persistent. Don't give in and continue doing it all because you won't be a happy homemaker.

It's All in the Flavor

It's easier to cajole him to do his share around the house than demand he go to work now. If you flavor your request with kindness, your husband will be more receptive. Constant nagging reminds me of a vulture. This bird of prey hovers until the carcass is weak, then picks away at the meat until there's nothing left. If you want your mate to do his share, don't henpeck him until there's no real desire on his part. Instead, flavor your message so he can see that he will actually reap the benefits of sharing the load.

Other Alternatives

Don't give up if you're having difficulty with your spouse coming around. As I said earlier, marital commitment is strongest when both partners receive as much as they give. You won't be happy if you continue doing it all when you don't want to. So persist, and let him know how much both of you stand to gain from the necessary change. In the meantime, there are other options for you. Sue Bowder says women need to learn to enjoy more relaxing moments instead of feeling like they always have to busily engage themselves in activity. A service business may be the answer for many overworked women and couples.

A potpourri of service businesses are available. You can hire people to do your laundry, keep your yard, even do your grocery shopping. Why you can even have gourmet dinners delivered to your door. One of the most popular services is housecleaning. Housekeepers no longer only come with 10,000 square feet mansions reserved for the rich and famous. You don't have to have a full-time maid. You can hire a service to clean your house daily, weekly, monthly, bimonthly, or even occasionally. The choice is yours. Use some of your hard-earned dollars to retain such a service.

Incidentally, Monogamous Male Seminar attendees receive a list describing "75 Ways To Romance Her" to give them new ideas and help them romance their love mates. One of the items on that list includes hiring a maid. After hiring a service they can take their mates out on the town for a much needed break. Though my husband does more than his share of the housework, he hired a cleaning service for my birthday. Believe me, it's a wonderful gift to receive. One married mistress says she and her husband recently hired a cleaning service to come in weekly. She says even with both of them sharing the workload, their weekends became overcrowded with housework, leaving little time for anything else. They decided they wanted to spend more time together and less time doing chores.

If you have children, they can and will help out. It benefits them to help out and teaches them responsibility. Errands divided between family members helps everyone.

Just *Stop* Doing It

Say you've always done everything in your household and you want some much needed help, but after all your coaxing and wheedling, your family refuses to do their share. As a last ditch effort, *just stop doing it!* If you have a husband who still lives in the Flintstone Age, refusing to pick up after himself, do dishes, or his fair share, simply stop being his maid. When your family and husband see you suddenly stop cleaning behind them, cooking their meals, or doing laundry they'll soon tire of the new "dirty" look. And when your husband demands to know why you stopped playing maid, look him directly in the eyes and calmly reply, "Superwoman doesn't live here anymore."

Superwoman Test

In your Married Mistress Workbook (see page 15), make a list of all the household chores you do daily and the approximate time each takes.

Write down how you would like your workload to change. (Realistically, of course.)

How much quality time do you spend with your spouse? (Daily)

How much more time would you like to spend together?

List the benefits your spouse would gain from sharing household duties.

Write a mini-talk you would give your husband to encourage him to split the household duties. Be sure to include the benefits he would receive.

Do you have room in your budget for a maid service or another convenience service? (You can enjoy this service even if your family pulls their weight because it gives all of you more time to do what you enjoy.) Call some services (look them up in the telephone Yellow Pages) and price them. Make sure you find a bonded agency (to cover any breakables, losses, or theft).

Begin planning a budget and see what you can afford. (Example, can you afford to hire a cleaning service monthly, bimonthly, etc.?)

monthly	bimonthly	weekly	biweekly
daily	occasionally		

Sixteen

For Me?

The Art of Receiving

Women are the nurturers of the world. As humble caretakers, they know all too well how to give, but how many women know how to receive? A common observation made by men who indulge in extramarital affairs was the disapproving way their wives routinely accepted gifts from them. They noted that their wives often reacted with disappointment or dissatisfaction when they received tokens of affection. One man took this even further when he insisted he preferred giving his mistress presents over giving them to his wife. He touts that his paramour showers him with appreciation, enthusiastically accepting her keepsakes with joy. On the other hand, he says his wife mumbles the usual, expressionless, "That's nice, dear," while neatly putting the item back in the box and asking if he kept the receipt.

Another Secret:

> The other woman is enthralled to receive gifts from someone else's man.

Whatever he does for her thrills her, whether it be sneaking off with her or showering her with trinkets because that means she is one step closer to whisking him away from his wife. Everything he does to show her he cares for her is another slap in the wife's face. And let's face it, the other woman sees the wife as the enemy; she has something the other woman wants--her husband.

Fatal Reaction

Mother's Day, birthdays, and wedding anniversaries are occasions most women greet with anticipation, (well, maybe not birthdays) while their mates frequently look at these dates with apprehension. "All our anniversary means to me is one more gift I have to pick out that she won't like," sighed one man. Sometimes, when a woman has too many negative reactions to her lover's gifts, the result is lethal to her gift-getting days.

Josie won't be getting any presents from her husband anymore. Dan hasn't bought his wife anything special for the last 20 of their 35 years of marriage. Josie had a negative reaction to the last gift Dan meticulously selected for her. Her biting response is what I call a *fatal reaction.* It demolished Dan's confidence to feel comfortable expressing his love for his wife with a suitable token from his heart.

"Mom desperately wanted a sewing machine," remembers Cindy, Josie and Dan's thirty-something daughter. "So dad thought he would surprise her with one for Christmas. He was so excited! He wrapped her gift ever so carefully, and he couldn't wait to see the look on her face when she opened it. He was like a kid, so giddy. When she did open it, she didn't say a word, but her face said it all--it wasn't the right model. As long as I live I will never forget the look of disappointment on my father's face--her reaction devastated him. It's been over twenty years, and he hasn't bought her a gift since. My brothers and sister and I try to encourage him to buy her things, but he won't. I don't know how many presents he had bought her before that, but I do know that one was definitely the last."

One attendee in a recent Married Mistress Seminar regretfully admitted she cried once when her boyfriend bought her a sensual lingerie set for her birthday. She remembers wanting a love poem instead. "I'll never forget how hurt he was by my tears. He told me that all he wanted to do was show me how beautiful I am by buying me something nice to wear. And all I could think about was what I didn't get. We broke up soon after that, and I've learned from that experience; in my marriage, I know to appreciate *any* gift my husband buys me as a show of his love."

To avoid suffering from a fatal reaction to presents you receive from your partner, learn how to welcome your gifts with love and appreciation. Accept them with genuine delight rather than thinking about what you wanted instead. Keep in mind the love and caring each present represents.

Man Watchers

A store clerk told me why she wishes department stores had a hidden booth where wives and girlfriends could watch their love mates shop for them. "The men put so much thought and time into their gift buying; it's sad to see their wives or girlfriends exchange the presents without a second thought. Some of those guys spend hours mulling over just the right gift. They are so meticulous when they shop for their women."

Sometimes women don't stop to think what they are saying to their significant others when they are so anxious to exchange those gifts. Many men give their partners cold, hard cash instead of taking the time to select something for their wives to reject. As one man put it, "This way, I'll save myself and her the trip."

Caught in the Act

When my son was five, he said something that made me laugh, but it also made me think. He was helping me bake a birthday cake for his older sister. I showed him how to use the hand-held beater to mix the batter and let him have his turn by himself. He was very excited and proud as he asked, "Am I doing it right, Mommy?" My response was quick;"Yes, you're doing it right, honey." Though I made sure to make my voice as cheerful sounding as possible, I couldn't help but envision the cake batter splattered all over the cabinets and refrigerator--all he had to do was slightly tilt the mixer the wrong way. My five-year-old immediately picked up on my nonverbals. He tilted his head to one side and innocently said, "But your face doesn't look like I'm doing it right." I had a good laugh, but I had to admit, he was right. I said he was doing it right, but my expression betrayed my words and told him I was putting up a front.

When receiving your gifts, if your mouth says, "For me? How

wonderful!" Make sure your face isn't saying,"The color is all wrong." If a five-year-old child can read facial signals, a grown man can undoubtedly spot a phony response. Sociologist Doris Wild Helmering contends that nonverbal communication in marriage is sometimes more significant than verbal communication. In her book, *Happily Ever After,* she says that nonverbal communication "plays a major role in the way couples let each other know what they are really thinking and feeling." Cindy's mother didn't have to say one word to tell her husband he bought her the wrong sewing machine--her face said it for her. Make sure your body language coincides with your positive reaction.

Fragile--Handle With Care

Looking at your gift, think about being in a private booth watching him shop for it. With your mind's eye visualize:

- ♥ The thoughtfulness that went into your keepsake,
- ♥ The time he spent pondering the perfect one for you,
- ♥ The love and tender emotion that's wrapped up with your token from the heart.

When you unwrap your gift, remember the positive sentiment, time, and tender care that went into this special package. The emotions wrapped up with your goodies are breakable. Instead of holding your present, pretend you are holding his ego in the palm of your hand. Though this package may not be marked, these words always apply: *Fragile--Handle With Care.*

Using your Married Mistress Workbook (see page 15), complete the following exercise:

Write a brief paragraph about your gift receiving habits. Analyze your past reactions to gifts from your love mate.

If you have ever received a gift and expressed that you wanted something else instead, write down that experience, and write down how you could have reacted differently.

Seventeen

Mom & Dad
Are a Couple

Keeping the Romance Alive A.C. (After Children)

Youngsters spoil romance. The spontaneous days of being a carefree couple become a thing of the past after children. And don't dare think about mentioning sex, that's out the door A.C. (after children). For many twosomes, those statements ring true. On the Maury Povich television talk show, Maury invited two couples to discuss how to keep the romance hot after marriage. One duo talked about their fantastic intimate relationship and how creating exciting escapades keeps their courtship sizzling. In sharp contrast, the other couple whined the entire time they were on stage, complaining about the lack of time for romance since the birth of their child. What struck me while I watched these people was the striking difference in their body language. The first couple held hands, smiled at each other, and almost acted as if they were in a private utopia, even though millions of people were watching. The other twosome was just the opposite. They barely made eye contact nor did they touch each other. They polarized themselves and blamed their lack of closeness on many things, including the responsibility of raising their child.

Many duos allow the task of raising their offspring to overburden their relationships. Marriage counselor Sonya Rhodes warns against allowing this to happen. In her column titled, "Why Perfect Mothers Make Lousy Lovers," she emphasizes that the bond between husband and wife should come "*before* the parent/child bond because the strength of your family depends upon you two as a couple." It is entirely possible and *essential* that you keep the romance blossoming after your children come into the world.

In an earlier chapter, I stressed the importance of thinking of your intimate bond as your first child. I reiterate the point here because it's vital to the well-being of your courtship. It's also an integral element in your marital affair. Neglecting your intimate relationship to raise your children allows the romance to grow cold. Dr. Paul Pearsall, author of *Super Marital Sex,* contends that just as many marriages fail because of children as children fail because of faulty marriages. He warns couples not to stifle their marriage or their individual development by always putting their children first. He also notes that as children, one of our biggest wishes is for our parents to be happy and suggests couples give their children that very gift.

You can easily find ways around the loss of spontaneity and create amorous moments to help nurture your intimate bond. Your ultimate goal is to raise your youngsters as a two parent family. If either one of you let the love become stale, you run the risk of growing apart.

Another Secret:

> The other woman wants you to put your children first. She wants you to forget about romance.

That way she can make her move. She wants you to disregard your intimate relationship because that represents another weak link in the marital chain she is willing to expose. While you are too busy with homework, PTA meetings, and girl scouts, she will always put him first. She makes sure she is available, especially when you are not.

Another reason she wants you to put your intimate bond on the back burner is so she can justify her actions. Most mistresses start out with a conscience. Most of them don't intentionally set out to sleep with someone else's mate. They don't plan to hurt the wife. However, they find it easier to lay their guilt aside by placing blame on the wife. A common rationalization mistresses had when interviewed was that most wives were too wrapped up in caring for the children, or other interests, to pay attention to their husbands. When they can fault wives for being neglectful, it becomes easier for them to bury their shame.

What About the Kids?

With a small amount of smart planning, you can spend quality time with your precious ones and put aside quality couple time. In a family with both parents working full-time, both of you have hectic schedules. By planning smart, you can give your youngsters the attention they deserve and still have time left to spend together. Let your children know you and your mate love each other and need couple time together. By communicating this early on, you teach them to expect you to do things as a couple and not always as a family. You also give them a good understanding of what a solid marital relationship is all about.

Start Small

The best time to keep your romance in the forefront is when your children are young. Starting with your first, get them into the habit of going to bed early so they get the adequate amount of rest they need. After safely tucking in your youngsters, use this time to cuddle and communicate with your beau.

Don't leave your kids out. Sit down and have a family dinner together as often as your schedules allow. After dinner, let your children have the floor. Give them each your complete attention. Let them tell you about their day at school. If you make this routine, your offspring will adapt and know that you will meet their need to spend time with mom and dad.

Another good time for conversing with your mate is when you arrive home after a hard day's work. Keep the lines open because there will be times when you need support from your mate after dealing with stress on the front-line of the work battlefield. He will, in turn, also seek your understanding shoulder. Always be there for each other. By introducing your need to spend time together early on, it will be easier for your youngsters to adjust.

No Trespassing

One good rule to establish in your house is to keep your bedroom your private place. A woman complained to me that she and her husband cannot enjoy intimate moments in their bedroom because her children are always there. She said she can't think of her bed as romantic anymore because there are always toys in it. If she and her husband let their children continue invading their bedroom any time they want, it won't be a romantic place.

Pediatrician William Sears offers argument for having what he calls a Family Bed, especially for the first two to three years of a child's life, to promote healthy parent/child bonding. A Family Bed is one where the parents and children all sleep together until the children feel comfortable sleeping in their own beds. While your children are young, there will be times (like when they experience frightening nightmares) when you will want to soothe their fears and allow them to sleep in your bedroom. However, you must nurture your couple bond as well as your sexual bond. A Family Bed can make this difficult. It's also difficult for the child to understand when to leave your bed if they sleep with you all the time. Some families interviewed by Dr. Sears who use the Family Bed admitted that sometimes their children were pre-teens or teenagers before they decided to move into their own beds. Nevertheless, some couples feel strongly about having a Family Bed. One suggestion is to locate the Family Bed in another room other than your bedroom. That way, when you and your mate want to nurture your couple bond, you have your bedroom as your private place.

Our youngsters come into our bedroom, but they understand that when our door is closed, they must knock before entering. We also afford them the same courtesy before entering their bedrooms. *Children learn respect easier if you teach it by giving them respect.* They are more apt to give you privacy if they know you won't invade their solitude. By teaching them to respect your privacy, you teach them manners but, at the same time, you teach them that you need time to be alone as a couple. When they become adults and get married, that respect will spill over into their own marital relationships.

Try a *DO NOT DISTURB* sign on your bedroom door to prevent young children from abusing their door knocking privileges. Sometimes a closed door is just too tempting. If they are too young to read, paint one side of the sign a different color, red for example, and let them know that when the sign is red, they must not knock unless it's urgent. You'll have to use positive reinforcement, especially if your children are young, but by consistently emphasizing your rules, and praising them when they follow them, they will catch on.

Show Them the Love

A forty-year-old woman once told me she never saw her

parents hug each other. She also confessed that it's hard for her to be affectionate with her husband. "I feel all closed up inside," she said sadly. "My husband doesn't think I really love him; I do, but I don't know how to show it." She isn't alone. Many parents don't show warmth toward each other in front of their children. They equate showing fondness for each other with teaching kids about sex. There's a difference. You can teach your children about affection without teaching them about sex.

Absence of tenderness toward your mate can make it hard for your children to share emotional moments with their significant others when they grow up. That's what happened to the woman who has trouble expressing her love to her husband. She never witnessed her parents' love for one another--they didn't even express it verbally. There's nothing wrong with showing your children that mom and dad love each other. In fact, some experts say it's even more important in today's society. Doug Fields, a national speaker and author of *Creative Romance,* says kids need to see "quality, loving relationships in a world where those aren't the norm." He notes that it's not uncommon for children to fear their parents may divorce, because divorce is prevalent among many of their friends' parents. He says that they may think it's only a matter of time before it happens in their own family. Visible evidence that you love each other can relieve your children's fears.

You can't share every tender moment you have with your spouse, but you can express your love for each other in many ways. Holding hands, hugging each other, and saying I love you reinforces that you belong together in your children's eyes. Too many people are unable to shelter their children from angry, emotional outbursts that are sometimes difficult to control. Yet, they take considerable measures to conceal expressions of their love for one another. What kind of message are they sending? Help your children understand that expressing love is not a sign of weakness or something undesirable--it's just another wonderful part of being human.

SHHHHH! The Kids Will Hear

Don't stop making love after children. Quelling the sweltering fires of desire until your children grow up and leave is not a viable bet. You will have to adjust your lovemaking. You may have to muffle those passionate screams of delight, but don't get into the trap of using the children as an excuse to stop making love. Instead, make love after they've gone to bed, or arrange for some afternoon delight while they're in school. Children don't keep people from having a healthy sex life. It just takes a little more planning. You can still enjoy some spontaneous romantic moments after children--it just calls for *planned spontaneity*. That means when you know you'll have some free time with your spouse, you leave the loving possibilities wide open.

Baby Sitters

What would we do without them? A good one is a gift from heaven. Good parenting is stressful. It calls for tenacity, patience, and consistency. Though you can't imagine ever getting irritated by the cute bundle of soft skin and dimples you bring home from the hospital, you're going to need a break from parenting regularly. If you have young children, one of the smartest things you can do to keep the burning fires of ecstasy lit is: *find a good sitter*. Living around extended family is a blessing if your relatives enjoy watching your kids. It saves you money and, more importantly, it prevents you from having to worry about things going awry with an inexperienced sitter.

Not living near family presents more of a challenge. You can meet that difficulty by taking needed precautions when selecting a good sitter. Above all, make sure it's someone your youngsters like and feel comfortable with. Also, make sure they are responsible enough to think of watching your little ones as a job. Always leave a number for the sitter to reach you and an emergency number of a close neighbor.

Getting Away From it All

There will probably be times when both of you want to escape from everyday life and create an amorous affair-like atmosphere that lasts a little longer than a few hours or one afternoon. Since we don't live near family, our situation presented a difficulty. We didn't feel a teenager was a good bet for keeping our youngsters overnight. We looked into hiring an overnight care agency, but the cost was high. We also felt uncomfortable leaving them with a stranger from an agency. Our solution was to fly my mother up to spend a week with the children and another week with us. It was a winning situation. Not only did she receive a free trip, she got a much wanted chance to spend time with her grandchildren. We also got a chance to spend time together as mother and daughter.

Alternatives include swapping with a neighbor. You keep

their kids when they go out-of-town and they reciprocate (the only drawback is when it's your turn). You could pay a good friend or neighbor to keep your children overnight. Another suggestion involves your day care. Sometimes child care workers will keep youngsters overnight. This gives you someone your little ones already know and gives the child care worker, who is usually immensely underpaid for the important job she holds, some extra pocket money.

Getting away for an extended romantic vacation calls for careful planning, but you can do it. After you do arrange to get away, the utmost item on your agenda is to *enjoy yourselves.*

Midlife Romance

As your youngsters grow up and go off to college woes of dirty diapers, hiring a sitter, and teenage temper tantrums will be behind you. Time for you to go through the empty nest syndrome, and time for dad to start going through his midlife crisis, right? *Not if you engage in a marital affair.*

Sure, you'll miss your children, and you'll be sad. Nevertheless, what you want to do rather than wallow is *get on with the romance!* Midlife is a splendid time for your marital affair. The spontaneity comes back to your relationship.

Midlife is a perfect time for you and your spouse to rekindle the kind of spontaneous romance you enjoyed before the children--it's time to revisit your youth--*together.* Embrace all the goodies yet to come your way. Travel together--date each other--indulge in each other. Savor every moment of your midlife courtship as if it was the first moment you laid eyes on each other. Become like strawberries discovering whipped cream for the first time. Dive in and devour your newfound freedom. Your marital affair will blossom!

Couple Time Exercise

1. Make plans to go out to dinner or do something romantic without the children. Arrange for someone to watch your youngsters, make reservations, etc. *Have fun.*

2. See how often you can fit a date with your love partner into your budget. Shoot for weekly or biweekly. If you are working with a tight budget, note the list below with several low-cost or free activities you can enjoy together.

3. Discuss and make plans to take an extended romantic holiday.

10 Low Cost Couple Getaways

♥ Enjoy a private picnic together.

♥ Take a Sunday drive one afternoon.

♥ Go on a $3.00 shopping spree. See what kind of goodies you can buy each other (things like gum, a romantic card, a pen or pencil, a favorite candy bar). Have fun finding a treasure trove of little love tokens for each other.

♥ Visit a local museum.

♥ Go out to eat for dessert.

♥ Take a romantic walk holding hands in the moonlight.

♥ Rent a couple of your favorite videos, pop some popcorn, curl up on the sofa, and watch them together.

♥ Get up early, and watch the breathtaking sunrise together.

♥ Take turns serving each other breakfast with one red rose in bed.

♥ Serve a delectable "midnight rendezvous" candlelight dinner for two.

Part III
The Sex Sextion

Eighteen

Why the Not Tonight Dear Syndrome Doesn't Exist for Mistresses

Mistresses don't get headaches. At least not when they're in the throws of an exhilarating lust affair with someone else's man. The vivid picture of the other woman most of us are familiar with finds her stretched out sexily on a sensuous bed with satin sheets draping her hot, perfumed flesh. She's anxiously anticipating her "date's" familiar knock on the hotel room door. And when he does, she lets him know she's ready for a night of erotic lovemaking. When he takes her in his arms, no way is she going to utter those words, "Not tonight dear, I have a headache."

No, the proverbial wife reserves those words for herself. Bob, who says his wife's attitude about sex played an intricate part in his infidelity, puts it this way: "After making love to a wet-rag once or twice a month, Nancy gives me the sexual excitement I've been craving. My wife sees sex as another one of her many duties. We definitely had a better sex life before we got married. Now she complains about not having enough energy for sex. And when I do finally get up the nerve to make a move on her to have sex, she lays there with no emotion at all. I almost feel guilty when I ask her for sex. With Nancy, sex is fabulous--she really wants me, and she loves it. She tells me over and over what a good lover I am. I was starting to worry that I was losing my touch, but Nancy let me know I haven't lost it yet--she's the best."

Schedule in Lovemaking?

Nancy doesn't have a bewitching spell on Bob. She does, however, understand the importance of reserving quality time for love. One of the most significant reasons the other woman always seems so eager to make love in that hotel room once or twice a week is because:

Another Best Kept Secret:

She schedules it in.

That point is paramount.

A friend of mine shared a story about a busy, high-level executive she knows who schedules in everything, including spending time talking to his four children. Everyday, he allots fifteen minutes for each child. He has his secretary schedule their appointments with him on his calendar. Now some may consider this far-fetched, having to write your children into your busy agenda. Yet, how many parents spend fifteen minutes every single day giving each of their children their *undivided* attention? Each of this executive's children receives fifteen minutes of dad's full attention, daily. No interruptions, no television blaring in the background, and no urgent telephone calls to compete with.

A University of Washington study points out that both the quantity and quality of sex is important to the well-being of your intimate relationship. Scheduling lovemaking takes care of both areas. It's essential to be in the right frame of mind when you're making love. I've heard more than one wife admit that sex is another obligatory chore they must perform in marriage. Believe me, if they think of sex as a chore, it will become one, and it won't be enjoyable for them or their mates. That's where scheduling in lovemaking works as an advantage. Most of us pencil in important events. Lovemaking is certainly as important as any dental appointment or social meeting. Yet, we painstakingly set aside time for these events and don't even consider setting aside *quality time to make love.* In a 1980 *Redbook* survey, couples noted that the sex topic they argued most about was the frequency of sexual intercourse. Couples can significantly reduce this argument by making it a point to take time out for lovemaking. Aren't you more receptive to your child reading you her new poem when you've already told her you'll sit down and listen after dinner? You aren't as receptive when you're in the middle of cooking dinner, while you're on the telephone, or whenever you focus your attention elsewhere. Lovemaking is no different. If you set aside quality time to relax yourself so you can enjoy a night of love with your beau, you mentally prepare yourself. Lovemaking won't be a chore because it will be more pleasurable for both of you.

Now I'm not suggesting that at eight every Wednesday night like clockwork, you're going to go into the bedroom and get it on. That would be too mechanical. Spontaneity is principal in good sex. Just take time out during the week to initiate some romance. It might be a nice, long intimate kiss that goes no further, or it may turn into a night of wildly passionate sex. By setting aside time for lovemaking, you enhance your sexual bond. *Having It All,* a book penned by Helen Gurley Brown encourages women to: "Be ready for love. That means you are juiced up, ready to go...with your *husband* most of the time, the way you were when you were single." She also strongly suggests women remember how they acted with a lover because, "husbands respond to that stuff, *too!*"

Scheduling Sex Reduces Stress

"When Tom calls me to tell me which hotel room to meet him in, I usually go an hour early so I can take a bath, get perfumed, and relax." That's what one mistress told me. She said the little time she spends with her married lover is so precious, they make sure to make the best of it.

What she's doing wrong is sleeping with someone else's man. But what she's doing right, making the best of their romantic time together, is what any woman can do. *That's one of the reasons the other woman attracts many married men.* To many of them, she offers an escape from life's everyday tensions. One man's comments are common of men who stray: "I go to see my girlfriend to escape. Escape from the noise of the kids screaming and my wife screaming at them. When I'm with Karen, she turns off the stressful sounds of the outside world." The other woman knows how to remove stress from her environment:

> **She makes sure there is no *stress* in being a mi*stress*.**

People wonder why the other woman is always so eager to make love. Well, she isn't *always* zealously available. She and her married lover steal an afternoon or evening to be together when they can. That makes this time a precious commodity. The other woman isn't about to waste these stolen moments on a headache. The only major difference between sex with her and typical sex with the proverbial wife is: *The other woman schedules it in.* That's how she eliminates the tension of not having time to make love.

As the wife, it's not always easy to remove stress. But how about as the married mistress? By espousing the role of a carefree married mistress, you can create the same stress-free environment that many married men hunger for. Engaging in a marital affair allows you to throw caution to the wind and temporarily forget your other duties. After all, isn't that what a married man does when he slips away to see the other woman? He escapes from everyday life. *While indulging in a marital affair, you become the seductive married mistress he escapes with.* It permits you to refocus and play the role of the sensuous mistress so you can momentarily stop worrying about:

- Your child's homework assignment,
- The never-ending pile of dirty clothes,
- What you're going to wear to work tomorrow,
- What you'll defrost for dinner,

and the 900 other things wives have on their minds.

Who says you can't call your husband on his job and ask him to meet you in room 205? Why can't you be the woman who arrives at the hotel an hour early to take that relaxing bath? And if you can't get away, you can always convert your bedroom into room 205. You can create the same ambience that the other woman offers in your own backyard.

Sex is a Great Stress Reliever

Writer Laura Flynn McCarthy straightforwardly emphasizes that everyday stress can lead to a variety of health problems. In her magazine article, "Stress-Busters That Work," she attests that these problems range "from acne to increased risk of heart disease." Too much stress is not good for the health of your intimate union, either. The other woman knows how to prevent everyday tensions from interfering with treasured intimate moments. After planning her romantic interlude, she usually relieves herself of any feelings of anxiety. When her lover pops up at her door, she's not going to waste time worrying about her broken down car, what meetings she has to attend this week, or a multitude of other worries she could allow to preoccupy her time. She wrestles with the same day to day headaches as any woman or wife. But she refuses to let her problems play interference with the time set aside to escape with her married lover.

Like stress, relief of it comes in an assortment of relaxation activities. One activity that relieves tension is: *Sex*. That's right. The one activity some wives try to avoid to keep from adding to their stress actually helps relieve it.

According to *London's Sunday Mirror*, sex benefits us in many ways:

- ♥ Kissing keeps wrinkles away. A passionate smacker uses 29 facial muscles. (*It feels good, too.*)
- ♥ Sex is great medicine for headaches. It causes the brain to release pain-killing chemicals.
- ♥ Making love burns 150 calories per hour. (*And you don't even have to worry about ruining any joints.*)
- ♥ Sex relaxes you mentally, helping to beat stress.
- ♥ Bedtime sex relaxes your muscles, helping you get a good night's sleep.

Adding to that, there's no better sleep aide I can think of than a dynamic orgasm. After you come down from the heavens, you'll sleep like a baby. So, take an important tip from the other woman, and make time for quality love. If you have to juggle your schedule and decide between having passionate sex with your man or doing laundry, do I have to tell you which one to postpone?

Twenty Ways to Relieve Stress

♦ Take a hot, relaxing bath.

♦ Indulge in your favorite hobby.

♦ Exercise is a great stress-buster.

♦ Have private quiet time.

♦ When you come home from work, don't immediately dive into chores. Take a relaxing breather first.

♦ Enjoy routinely scheduled outings by yourself.

♦ Regularly engage in couple outings without the children.

♦ Treat yourself to a professional massage.

♦ Give yourself permission to make mistakes. Being a *perfect wife calls for a stressful life.*

♦ Split the household chores. (Covered in detail in Chapter 15.)

♦ Go on a fun shopping spree alone or with a friend. Only buy things for yourself.

♦ If you don't feel like doing it, DON'T! (Chores can always wait.)

♦ Plan ahead. (As we know, planning and scheduling is helpful in many ways.)

♦ Take a relaxing walk.

♦ Take deep breaths. If you find yourself going into a stressful situation, like speaking in front of others (the activity people fear most), taking a few deep breaths helps calm you down.

♦ Don't spread yourself too thin. Learn to be assertive and delegate. Practice saying no.

♦ Treat yourself to a new fashion, or hairdo.

♦ Learn to make notes to yourself. This will help relieve the stress of forgetting little things like picking up salt at the grocery store.

♦ Read a spicy novel.

♦ Last, but certainly not least; *enjoy delightful SEX with your mate.* (You didn't think I'd forget that one did you?)

Scheduling Exercise

In your Married Mistress Notebook (see page 15), complete the following exercise:

1. Write down your daily schedule.

2. Roughly determine the number of times a week you'd like to make love.

3. Like the mistress, mentally work it into your schedule. And make it fun--create a seductive ambience.

4. Make love to your man as his seductive married mistress.

5. Practice this exercise (especially number 4) on a regular basis.

6. Occasionally live out your marital affair in a romantic hotel room. Meet each other there as two passionate lovers who have garnered a few stolen moments.

Nineteen

Sex and the Married Mistress

Sexual Inhibitions

The previous chapter discussed the importance of scheduling time to make love. But one reason some people avoid lovemaking is because of negative values they associate with the act. This chapter addresses the importance of overcoming sexual inhibitions.

Even in the contemporary world we live in with its supposed sexual openness, puritanical sexual attitudes crawl into bed with many married couples, haunting and inhibiting their sex lives.

In their book about *Sex And Human Loving,* Masters and Johnson affirm that this society still lives with the "sex is dirty" legacy and with the innate sense of secrecy about an act to be practiced in secret and rarely enjoyed. Many married couples allow negative messages to override the pleasure they derive from sexual intercourse. This chapter discusses ways these messages can interfere with a well-rounded marital relationship. A good sexual attitude is an integral part of a flourishing marital affair.

The "Married People's Bed"

John, a middle-age firefighter, has enjoyed an exciting love affair with Marie, his married mistress and partner for over two years. But John had a first-hand experience with jumbled up ideas about intercourse with his first wife.

"While I was dating my first wife, she was wonderful. We had fun times together, and we had great sex. I made this sensual bed for us with my own two hands--it had drapes for privacy, a mirror on the ceiling, plus a built-in stereo system. I made the entire bed out of rich mahogany wood. We had wild sex in that bed--she loved it. Well, at least, I thought she did. About a week after we tied the knot, I was breaking down the bed, section by section, so I could move it into our new apartment. I was being extremely careful to break it down without damaging it; I was anxious to get it moved. I carefully numbered each section so the pieces would be easier to reassemble." He paused for a moment, the image of what happened years ago still fresh in his mind.

"So what happened?" I interjected.

"Well, she came into the bedroom and asked me what I was doing. I told her why I was breaking down the bed. She looked directly at me, and without blinking an eye, told me I was not moving that bed into our new place. I asked her why, and she said married couples slept in what she called a 'married people's bed'--not a bed for having sex. She stunned me--less than one week before, she was enjoying having sex in that same bed! I didn't think anything had changed; just days before we got married, we were enjoying the hell out of ourselves in that bed. Then, as soon as I put the ring on her finger she sees that kind of sex as something married people don't enjoy. I had no idea she even felt that way. She never said anything to indicate her feelings. And me? Well, I thought we were the same two people who had been screwing our brains out in that bed. All we did different was get married, but I didn't think that changed us as people. I didn't even know there was such a thing as a bed for married people--did you?"

John said he and his wife fell right into their "married" roles after that. He said she reacted angrily when he tried to do his own laundry, feeling that was her responsibility. "The marriage only lasted ten months," admitted John. I've learned from the experience that it's better to lay all the cards on the table up front. My live-in lover, Marie, and I have an exhilarating sexual relationship, and you can bet that this time, I made sure she wasn't the type of woman who would change her views after I moved in with her."

John's first wife seemed to think uninhibited sex was O.K. for two people who were dating. The minute she became John's wife, however, she felt there was something tainted about enjoying healthy sex even though, as individuals, neither of them had changed. Somehow in her mind, she completely separated good sex from married sex.

Sex Is Not a Four-Letter Word

Matrimony offers many people the perfect excuse for not

having good sex. Think about it. Why is it that when birth control is more readily available to teenagers than it has ever been, teenage pregnancies are in record numbers? According to Planned Parenthood, one million American teenage girls get pregnant every year.

When a young girl about to go on a date with her boyfriend visits the clinic to seek birth control, she's admitting she may have sex. If she believes good girls don't, she views enjoying sex as something bad. So she goes into denial and neglects to protect herself. By being without protection, she can say succumbing to her bodily urges was an unplanned accident, just like her pregnancy. Teenage pregnancy is a high price to pay for sexual denial.

Marriage says it's O.K. to have sexual intercourse any time you want. However, when you learned to deny your sexual desires, it's not that easy to suddenly believe intercourse is all right. Thus, when we marry, many times we make excuses not to enjoy sex. The old tapes reminding us that sex is dirty still play in the back of our minds.

"My parents never talked about it. I always thought it was something no one ever did, unless they wanted kids."

"I know it's not supposed to be something you enjoy. That's what my parents told me."

"Whenever my mom talked about 'it' she had this scowl on her face. I just can't shake the feeling that sex is dirty."

"I think one of the hardest things for both my husband and me was to turn off the old message about sex being something filthy. How can you after your parents tell you all your life it's something you avoid? To try to tell yourself it's O.K. after marriage is difficult."

Those kinds of comments came up frequently during interviews with married couples. Most of them have, at one time or another, grappled with the idea that sex is something dirty. Putting that attitude to rest poses a challenge for some couples, but conquering sexual inhibitions offers many rewards.

A common denominator in overcoming sexual inhibitions is overcoming the guilt associated with the act. Dr. Wayne W. Dyer, author of the best selling book, *Your Erroneous Zones*, notes that the area where guilt flourishes best is in sex. He says if he had to locate a guilt center in the body, he'd place it in the crotch. Overcoming deeply embedded guilt associated with sex is difficult, but the guilt is conquerable.

The marital affair breeds the perfect environment for a healthy sex life. David Hajdu affirms that good sex is an outward sign of a strong inner relationship. In his magazine article, "How To

Prevent Divorce," he advises couples to keep the sex sizzling. There's nothing obscene about indulging in rewarding lovemaking with your love partner. In fact, a healthy sexual life is an integral part of any intimate relationship.

Sex at the Dining Room Table

So how do you go about turning around negative sexual messages? You can start by realizing that: *good sex doesn't begin in the bedroom.* It begins with communication. To improve the action in the bedroom, you and your mate must talk about it before anything takes place. Talking openly about sexual attitudes helps bridge any sexual gaps the two of you may have. Remember that John's ex-wife shocked him when he discovered how she viewed sex for married people. He admitted sex was something they never really discussed.

Talking about sex in a neutral corner such as the dining room table, or in the living room where you can sit apart and look each other in the eye is important. Sexual tensions tend to run high in the bedroom. Any negative comment uttered during sex can literally "kill the mood." The best time to discuss any sexual concerns or inhibitions with your mate is: *when you are not having sex.*

If you feel guilty about sex or are experiencing other negative messages, discuss them with your mate. You may even need to seek professional help. Talking openly about why you feel more comfortable doing it with the lights off, or why you avoid making love, can help your partner understand that you're not rejecting him, but you're working at dealing with your sexuality. Sam, one of the men engaged in a marital affair with his wife, credits being able to talk about his negative sex messages as the turning point in their sexual relationship. Sexual awareness goes a long way in a solid intimate union.

Your Biggest Sexual Organ Is Not in Your Pants

It's in your head. That's right--good sex is all in your mind. If you think of sex as something good girls don't do or as something lewd, that's exactly what it will be for you. On the other hand, if you look at it as a sensual adventure to deepen your intimate bond with your mate, that's what it will become for both of you. Good sex, fulfilling sex, is a deep and affectionate expression of the love you share for one another. A beautiful act of becoming one with each other. It's the most rewarding and meaningful act of intimacy you can share with him. A recent study by Dr. Steven Gold and psychologist David Chick confirms that individuals who have a healthier mental attitude about sex get more involved in fantasizing and enjoying good sex.

Good sex is also good for you. Dr. Barbara De Angelis calls the sexual act powerful because "it is the closest we ever come to uniting with another being." In her book, *How To Make Love All The Time,* she says sex is important to your intimate bond because "it's physically satisfying, it creates more intimacy and closeness, and a healthy sex life builds up your self-esteem."

Eight Ways to Enhance Your Sexuality

♦ Reprogram your guilt messages with messages of intimate closeness and sexual self-esteem. Place your focus on how good sex feels with your partner.

♦ Remember, good sex doesn't start in the bedroom--it begins with communication.

♦ Think of yourself as a well-rounded sexual being. It involves much more than the act of intercourse. It means building intimacy, feeling good about yourself, and learning how to communicate your sexuality.

♦ Deal with any sexual guilt you may harbor. If you need to, seek a professional therapist.

♦ Spend intimate time with your partner. This doesn't mean always using this time to engage in the act of sexual intercourse. A sense of intimacy and closeness with your partner helps build sensuality.

♦ Take responsibility for your sexual satisfaction. It's not only up to your partner to satisfy you sexually. Taking an active role will enhance your sex life.

♦ Don't work too hard at having good sex. Don't turn sex into hard labor. The harder either of you try at sex, the more tense you become, pushing sexual pleasure further away and adding to an already uptight situation. Relax and take it one step at a time.

♦ Enjoy yourself. Remember, whatever you and your mate do in the privacy of your sexual relationship is your business, and there is only one goal in mind--*mutual sexual satisfaction.*

Assessing Your Sex Life

In your Married Mistress Workbook (see page 15), please answer the following questions as honestly as you can.

1. On a scale of one to ten (ten being the best) how would you rate your sex life?

2. Are you conservative when it comes to sex?

3. Would you like to open up more sexually?

4. Is your partner passive, assertive, or overly aggressive when it comes to sex?

5. Do you have a high, low, or medium sex drive?

6. Does your mate have a high, low, or medium sex drive?

7. When you are on different sexual clocks (example: he wants it more often than you do) how is the situation typically resolved? Do you half-heartedly give in, does he stomp away in anger, etc.?

8. Is it difficult to talk to your mate about sex? If yes, why?

9. Have you ever divulged a sexual fantasy to your mate? If no, why not?

10. What could your mate do to improve your sex life?

11. What could you do to improve your sex life?

12. Do you play "Follow The Leader" when you and your mate have sex? (In other words, you follow his lead even if what he's doing doesn't satisfy you.)

Twenty

He Said/She Said

He Said

"I know I satisfy her every time we have sex. Yeah, I give it to her real good," he lines his words with cockiness. "Her moans of pleasure tell me all I need to know. I've never had any problem satisfying a woman. It's pretty easy, really--you just get in a little foreplay, rub in all the right places, if you know what I mean." "He" laughs then goes on. "Then you get busy--next thing you know, she can hardly control herself. 'She' comes every time. I know I satisfy her."

She Said

"Does 'He' satisfy me? Well, (pregnant pause) most of the time, I guess he does. I mean, 'He' makes all the right moves, but sometimes, I don't know, it feels so, uh, mechanical. I don't want to hurt his feelings so I just pretend--a lot. Sometimes I wish he'd slow down a bit. He rushes the foreplay so he can get right into having intercourse. But, (pauses) I wish he'd... (her voice trails) well, I guess I wish he'd slow down a little more. Other than that, yeah, 'He' satisfies me."

Sexual Views

Two people engaged in the same sexual activity often have polarized accounts of it. When "He" confidently bragged about satisfying his wife in bed, his over-inflated ego did a lot of the talking. From puberty, men learn that satisfying a woman is easy, especially if they warm her up beforehand. But as "He" described foreplay as rubbing a little in all the right places, it's evident that he doesn't understand what it is. He's been doing what most males in the locker room do upon discovery of their anatomy--bragging about how to satisfy a woman. Most men are lead to believe it takes little effort.

After hearing her version, it's clear that she's putting up a front. It's also apparent that "She" isn't sure what she wants herself. "He's" not completely at fault for his overblown ego. "She" shares the blame by not being honest about what she wants in bed. This is difficult for her is because though "She" knows what she doesn't want, it's harder for her to pen down what she does want him to do to turn her on. "She's" not in touch with her own body. Lesley Dormen's magazine article, "Honey, You're A Great Lover...Not!" confirms that her reaction is typical of the average married woman. Dormen says most married women have lied to their husbands about their lovemaking skills. In Dormen's article, sex therapist Judith Siefer warns that women need to let their husbands know the truth. "If you don't speak up, your husband will assume he's doing it right."

Bedroom Actress Satisfied With Applause

DEAR ANN LANDERS: Hurrah for the gal who signed herself "Honest." I'll bet the true number of bedroom Sarah Bernhardts in this world would be a shock--even to you. Yes, I am one of the vast army of actresses.

Why do we do it? Because we love our men and don't want them to feel inadequate. We accept the fact that we have been biologically short-changed by Mother Nature and that isn't anybody's fault. No woman ever enjoys sex as much as a man does and she never will. So we just go on doing our little act. Knowing that our men are satisfied is enough for us. Do you have the guts to print this? ENJOYING NOTHING BUT THE APPLAUSE IN KANSAS CITY.

DEAR KC: If the applause is all you're enjoying, you are gypping yourself plenty. Your basic theory is incorrect, and I hope you will have the guts to discuss your problem with a therapist so you can begin to experience what is rightfully yours.

As Ann Landers points out, it is a woman's right to seek sexual satisfaction. Lying to your mate results in unwarranted denial of pleasure.

It's Your Orgasm

Like many women, "She" knew what turned her off. However, discovering her sexual hot-button takes a little more effort. A woman in tune with her body can better pin-point what turns her on. "He" was correct when he included foreplay in his short description of sex. However, Webster defines foreplay as *sexual stimulation preceding sexual intercourse.* Like the definition, the act encompasses more than "rubbing in the right places." As a woman, you must determine what kind of sexual stimulation pleases you. Do you like your back rubbed, what about your breasts--your thighs? Do you enjoy him licking your ear, or does it feel like something wet and sloshy lurking around where it doesn't belong? These are the kind of questions you need to answer so you can lead him down the right path to your sexual enjoyment.

Good Sex = Communication

Good lovemaking is not innate. There are two entities unique to your sexual union--*you and your partner.* Together, it's up to both of you to create the kind of physical bond that is mutually satisfying. Leaving it up to fate, or mimicking experience with past partners is not good enough. The best way both of you can enjoy sex is by following this simple rule:

•Tell each other what you want.

"When my husband and I got married, he asked me what I like in bed, and I told him just do whatever it is you do," confessed one married mistress. "I didn't know what to say." Her response is typical of women who find it embarrassing to discuss the subject with their partners or who assume everyone makes love the same way.

Dr. Johnathan Kramer and Diane Dunaway, co-authors of *Why Men Don't Get Enough Sex And Women Don't Get Enough Love,* note that since differences between men and women are so vast when it comes to sexual intercourse, it is essential to communicate sexual needs. As one monogamous male puts it, "Men and women do all that talking to get into bed together; it shouldn't stop when the sex starts."

"Husbands Are Lousy Lovers," a magazine article that appeared in *Ladies Home Journal,* had respected sex therapist Helen Singer Kaplan M.D., Ph.D., confirming that most men want to be good lovers. She acknowledges that men are not selfish; they just don't know what to do or how to do it. Some women assume their partners don't care about pleasing them, but many men don't know how. They need input from their partners--that's where communication comes in.

Sexually, a man is like a microwave oven, and a woman is more like a conventional oven. Men are quick to warm up while most women need more stimulation to build up to the act of intercourse. Renee says she finally had to tell her husband not to grab at her while they were having sex. "After my kids have clawed at me all day, I don't want him clawing at me at night and grabbing at my clothes so we can get right into having sex--I want him to make love to me. Now that I've told Alan, he's surprisingly romantic. He sets the mood by changing the ambience in the den, where I've encapsulated myself all day with our baby daughter. He cleans up her toys and lays out comfortable throw pillows and lights romantic candles--then he makes sweet and gentle love to me. He makes me feel so wonderful. If I hadn't spoke up, he never would have known how I felt. He'd still be grabbing at me thinking it was turning me, on and it would still annoy me."

Had Renee neglected to speak up, assuming that her needs weren't important to Alan or that her sexual satisfaction was secondary to his, she never would have discovered what an attentive sexual partner she has. It turned out Alan had no idea how Renee felt, and as soon as she gently, but firmly, made her feelings clear to him, he was quick to respond by becoming a more tender lover.

Writer Bob Berkowitz affirms that most men feel sex is almost a failure if the woman does not have an orgasm. Men want to please their partners in bed--it's up to their women to show them how.

It's Delicious!

Having trouble expressing yourself during sex? When speaking up during lovemaking are you as quiet as a church mouse? Here's a suggestion that helps quell the embarrassment of sexual expression. Just pretend you're eating the most delicious dessert of your choice. When you're tasting something that especially pleases your palate, it's not hard to make yummy sounds like, "MMMMM," or "Boy, is that good." Well, that's all there is to sexual expression. If it feels good, make a yummy sound.

Five Delicate Ways to Say, It Doesn't Turn Me On.

1. **Don't say anything.**
   Your silence will be a signal to him that he hasn't hit your hot button yet.

2. **I like that better.**
   When he ventures into territory that gives you more pleasure, let him know.

3. **I *really* like it when you do that.**
   Reinforce him doing it again and again.

4. **Oh, *this* feels so good.**

5. **Let's try this.**
   If he doesn't hit your hot spot, lead him to it.

Tell Me What You Want

Lovemaking is supposed to offer mutual gratification for both of you. If it doesn't, you need to speak up. But how do you tell him what satisfies you when you don't really know yourself? You must know your own body. The next chapter covers the importance of body awareness. Exciting and gratifying sex plays a major role in a good marital affair. Learning to explore your sexual horizons together promises no dull moments in your sensual liaison.

Twenty Ways To Tell Him He's Doing It Right

1. MMMMMMMmmmmmmmmmmmm.

2. That is soooo good!

3. You are the best!

4. I *love* it when you do that.

5. More, More!

6. Oh, Baby!

7. Yes! Yes!

8. Boy, you're good!

9. Right there.

10. *I LOVE IT!*

11. Do that again!

12. Don't stop.

13. Oh, Yeah.

14. I love you.

15. That's just what I needed.

16. You're so good to me.

17. You're the best lover!

18. Let's do that again!

19. You make me feel sooooo good.

20. I want you.

Twenty-One

Body Language

Most extramarital affairs start with a sexual bang. Good sex may not be what keeps a man adulterous, but it plays a part, especially at the onset of the affair. The affair usually enjoys a variety of episodes of wildly passionate sex. That same sensual excitement is a reality in a marital affair. To benefit both of you, mutual satisfaction has to occur. That satisfaction comes from open and honest sexual communication. That means knowing your body and communicating what makes you feel good.

The G-Spot Theory

There's another important reason you need to know your body. It is easy for misinformation in magazine articles and books to mislead a man in his quest to sexually satisfy his partner. For example, according to some sexual theorists, inside every woman exists a small patch of tissue known as the G-spot (named after Dr. Ernest Grafenberg, its original discoverer). These theorists claim that when properly stimulated by intense pressure, this G-spot leads to an earth-shattering orgasm or series of such. Many sex therapists argue the validity of such a spot existing at all. Some women swear it does. The problem I have with this theory is the way Grafenberg suggests men locate a woman's G-spot. *Intense* pressure is the key. His instructions call for a man to put his finger inside and curl it so the tip hooks behind a woman's pubic bone, then pretend he is about to pick her up with that finger. "The pressure is that strong," he says.

I don't know about you, but I'm not real anxious for my

husband to apply that kind of pressure to find something I'm not so sure is really there. During sexual intercourse, that kind of pressure calls for serious thrusting on a man's part, which can be very painful. In her magazine article, "When Sex Hurts," Dava Sobel verifies that though a woman may experience varying degrees of pleasure ranging from mild to ecstatic, sex should not be painful.

"I couldn't figure out why Jerry was thrusting so hard during intercourse, says Roberta, who took the Married Mistress Seminar. It felt like he was trying to put a hole in my intestines--it hurt. He finally told me one day that he had read about this G-spot and how it makes a woman have an uncontrollable orgasm. I told him what I was having wasn't coming close to an orgasm, just more like wildly intense pain. I told him I didn't think I had a G-spot and asked him to please stop trying to find it. I liked our sex the way it was. He didn't need to try anything he read in a magazine. After that, we went back to having the gentle kind of sex we used to have-- the kind I like. I don't know who this guy is that's telling these men about our so called G-spot, but I wish he was a female and someone was applying all that pressure to find his. I wonder how insistent he'd be on saying it exists in that case. When Jerry was doing all that thrusting and causing me pain, all he did was thrust me entirely out of the mood for having sex."

Different things turn different women on sexually. Don't let any theory or study mislead you to believe you lack something if you don't reach climax the way other women do.

Most men want to please their sexual partners. As Jerry did, it's not unusual for a man to read a magazine article or book about how to satisfy a woman and then try a new method out on his lover. The only problem with this is that each woman's sexual makeup is varied--like the mixture of perfumes on a vanity. The best person to tell your man how to satisfy you in bed *is you.*

Twenty-Two

Fantasies Fulfilled

Whether we admit it or not, we all have sexual fantasies. What man doesn't secretly fantasize about having vivacious sex with a woman who can't keep her hands off him? That's why extramarital liaisons attract many men like magnets to steel. Unfortunately, this kind of fantasy, when played out in an extramarital affair, reeks havoc in marriages. But when you bring that same fantasy to life in a *marital affair* the possibilities are oh, so delectable!

Meet Me in Room 205

"We both needed some rest and relaxation, so I took the advice you gave in the Married Mistress Seminar. I made hotel reservations for Friday night, lined up the kids' sitter, and bought a sexy teddy--a red one.

"After the sitter arrived, I went to the hotel. I also packed some of Ted's things. When I got to the room, I took a hot, relaxing bath, did my makeup a bit more daring, and slipped into my skimpy teddy. I took a deep breath and made the call to Ted at work. He had about an hour left on the job. I made my voice as seductive sounding as I could, and said something like:"

Hi Babe, I finally managed to get away from my hectic schedule. I have a whole evening free. I'm at the Hyatt in Room 205, and I'm waiting for you. Meet me here as soon as you get off. I can't wait to see you. I want your body so badly I can hardly stand it!

"That's about what I said. I couldn't believe those words were coming from me! Anyway, Ted was speechless. He took a few heavy breaths, and all he said was, 'O.K.'

"I swear, within forty-five minutes, Ted was knocking on my hotel room door. He never leaves work early, but he did that day. When I opened the door and he saw me in my sexy outfit, I think he thought he had the wrong room. I quickly grabbed him and pulled him in. We made love three or four times that night. That whole fantasy, the whole set-up turned both of us on--we hadn't made love like that in years!"

Don't Down Play It--Play It Out

Megan is a smart lady. Instead of chastising Ted for fantasizing about an erotic episode in a hotel room, she enjoyed the fantasy with him. That's what is so wonderful about the marital affair. It gives you license to carry on a tantalizing love affair with your mate. Instead of denying or suppressing these sensual fantasies, you can embrace and indulge in them. A study appearing in *The Journal of Sex Education and Therapy* surveyed 86 men and 115 women to learn more about sexual fantasies. The study showed that the majority surveyed felt comfortable giving themselves permission to enjoy sexual fantasies. Masters and Johnson call fantasies "the best aphrodisiacs you can find." They say that your imagination can "help you transform ordinary sex into something far more stimulating."

Female Fantasies

Marie, a married mistress, admits that having a marital affair with her live in lover is like having multiple sex partners in one body. "If I want to pretend I'm having sex with the postman, we create that fantasy. It's great, and our sex is never boring. My fantasies don't intimidate John because he knows in the end it's him I sleep with, no one else. If I didn't act out these fantasies with John, I wouldn't act them out at all."

Another married mistress chuckles as she expresses one of her favorite fantasies. Alan (her husband) pretends like he's the handyman coming to fix her plumbing. "We have to make love in a hurry before my 'husband' gets home," she laughs. Sherri, another married mistress, admits the fantasy she and her husband enjoy whenever they can is making love in the back seat of their car. And

Terry made her fantasy come true when she secretly video taped an "afternoon delight" lovemaking episode with her husband. She sprung the tape on him that night after dinner, and he loved it!

I'm So in *Lust* With You

A common fantasy shared by many men is visualizing their women aggressively seeking their erotic pleasures from them. More than one man interviewed admitted that they enjoy their wives making the moves on them for some good loving. "When I know she wants me," says one man, "it makes sex better for me." Nevertheless, many women find themselves somewhat inhibited by their view of lusting after someone. In the magazine article "Sexual Ecstasy," women interviewed admitted that they view lusty women as whores. Writer Linda Murray describes lust as a "combination of passion, laughter, urgency, pleasure, eroticism, and freedom." She calls lust an "essential component of sexual ecstasy."

There's absolutely nothing wrong with lusting after your mate. Think about it from his point of view. When you want him to kiss you, you want your man to sweep you up in his arms and plant the most passionate smacker on you. If he reacted like he barely wanted to touch you and looked at you as if he's thinking, "All right, let's get this over with," you'd be disappointed. When you want love, knowing the person wants your love makes all the difference, doesn't it? Well, that's exactly the way most men feel. By showing your man you're in absolute *lust with him*, you're showing him you want him. Nothing is sexier to a man than that.

Understanding Men

When it became known I was teaching couples how to put more excitement in their marriages, I had an interesting conversation with a business executive I'd known for awhile. He had read a newspaper story about the Married Mistress Concept. In the story, one feminist who did not fully understand the concept criticized me for teaching women to be subservient to men. David quickly defended the idea. "That woman is way off base," he told me. "I, like most men, understand exactly what you're doing. You're teaching married people to make the most of what they've got." He then spent the next thirty minutes talking about his wife and their fantastic marriage.

He told me how she made a big splash on their wedding anniversary one year. With the help of his supervisor, his wife cleared his schedule for the Friday afternoon before their anniversary. She booked a hotel room and pre-ordered room service. Then she showed up at his job in a trench coat, took him in his office, closed his door, and removed her coat, revealing the sexy, black bustier and garter with black stockings underneath. When they arrived at the hotel room, she had flowers and balloons all over the room and chilled champagne waiting for them. The glow this straight-laced business executive had on his face as he re-lived this memory was evidence of his appreciation of his wife's showering of love. Though it happened a few years back, when he brags about it, it's as if it happened yesterday. He said it's something he'll never forget, and all he could think of was what he could do to come close to making her feel as special as she made him feel. And when the other executives in his office grunt and groan about their lack-luster love lives, that's his cue to share his story about one wonderful fantasy fulfilled with the woman of his dreams--*his wife*. "The men I tell are green with envy," he touts as his chest puffs up with pride.

Since starting the Married Mistress and Monogamous Male Concepts, I've had men call my office to say thanks. As one man put it, "Thank you for telling me it's O.K. to have an affair with my wife. I've always wanted our relationship to be more exciting, I didn't want to cheat, but sometimes, it did cross my mind. This way, I can have my fun in our love affair and I'm not hurting my wife or sneaking around with another woman. Where were you five years ago? This is wonderful!"

Making the most of your intimate relationship is something most men fully understand. We all have fantasies. Share them with your mate. Encourage him to share his with you. The more fulfilling and stimulating both of you make your marital sex life, the closer your sexual bond will become. This bond is one more unbreakable link in your marital chain.

Fantasy Exercise

In your Married Mistress Workbook (see page 15), write down two or three of your most sensual fantasies. Explore them with your mate.

Twenty-Three

75 Ways to Spice Up Your Love Life!

Romantic at Heart

I knew what he wanted when I saw his masculine frame hovering over me while I lie in my bed. His eyes spoke of heated desire as he slowly undressed my delicate body with his long, yearning look. It was as if he was searching for the key to unlock my wall of forbidden lust, and let him in.

I turned my head slowly, allowing my eyes to meet his. The slinky turquoise chemise I was wearing had molded itself gracefully around my protruding breasts. My breathing was quick and shallow. I felt the rushing waters of my passion about to overtake me. I wanted to wade in this sinful liaison with Michael, exploring every inch of his beautifully bronzed frame. His muscular chest was seductively peeking out of his unbuttoned shirt.

As I slowly stood he gently surrounded me with his arms--his hot breath on my face. I was dizzy with desire. I didn't know how much longer I could fight off my feelings for Michael. Gently, he caressed my face with his hand and moved his face toward mine to meet my lips with his.

His kiss was long and passionate, as his tongue searched every longing corner of my wet, hungry mouth. I was weak with yearning--doomed to love a man I could not have. I stopped kissing Michael and sadly uttered, "This isn't right."

Michael looked puzzled. "You know I want you. I thought you felt the same way," he said, his voice yearning. I felt lost. I knew I loved Michael, and he knew it, too. I was torn between what was right and what I knew in my heart I wanted. It was time to tell Michael the truth. At last, in a whisper, I uttered my final decision...

KNOCK. KNOCK. The knock on the door rips Judy's attention away from her romance novel.

"Here I come baby, are you ready for a night of passionate lovemaking with your one and only? Her husband opens the bedroom door and peeks in, anticipating her eagerness for a night of romance.

"Darn you, Joe!" "Can't you see I'm right in the middle of this romance novel?!" She heaves the words at him, angry that he would dare interrupt her while she reads about someone else's romance. "Please don't interrupt me again! I want to find out what Teal says to Michael! You just don't understand anything about romance." She hisses impatiently and buries her head in her novel, ignoring Joe. He looks at her in wonderment, then looks hurt. His manhood drops suddenly as he leaves her to snuggle up with her novel.

That sounds like an outrageous scenario, but I've talked to women who are more in touch with steamy novels and soap operas than with their own romantic episodes. One of the best ways to enhance your love life is to create the same type of atmosphere depicted in romance novels in your own relationship. Romance novels serve as food for your appetite for love. They whisk you away to the most romantic corners of the world and weave you into fever-pitched love affairs with beautiful people. They're a fabulous motivation for creating some of those same fantasies with your real fantasy man-- your love mate.

The following suggestions are 75 ways to keep those love fires burning bright:

1. **Kidnap him and whisk him away for a romantic night in a hotel.**
    Prearrange for a sitter, pack your clothes in the trunk of the car, and take off! This is a great way to get away from it all. An overnighter in a hotel without the kids is a refreshing way to renew your romance and get in some precious couple time. If you feel you can't fit this into your budget, put aside a little money every payday in a "couple fund." Use this money to create these little escapades.

2. **Give him a big hug and kiss when he leaves for work in the morning.**
    Give him something to look forward to when he comes home.

3. **Get dressed in a trench coat (nothing underneath), get a toy gun, walk up to him and say, "Hi, I'm Dirty Harriet, and I'm here to MAKE YOUR DAY."**
    This one is sure to get a rise out of your man.

4. **Let him serve you breakfast in bed.**
Remember, it's a two-way deal. Encourage him to do things like this for you by praising him whenever he does something special for you.

5. **Serve him breakfast in bed.**
This makes him feel special, too.

6. **Take a walk in your neighborhood holding hands.**
Another way to hold on to the things you did while dating each other.

7. **Play his *French Maid*.**
Dress up in a sexy maid costume, and let him help you make the bed. (I'm sure you'll get very little objection from him on doing this bit of housework.)

8. **Go on a honeymoon overnighter or weekender to rekindle the wedding night romance.**
You don't have to be newlyweds for this one because if you're having a marital affair, *your honeymoon is one that never really ends.*

9. **Go out on a date.**
For this one you'll need to get dressed at a friend's house so your beau won't see what you're wearing. Then have him pick you up--just like you did when you were courting.

10. **Encourage him to divulge one of his intimate sexual fantasies.**
Remember, the best way to keep your sex life healthy and active is to live out fantasies together.

11. **Divulge one of your romantic fantasies to him.**
We all have them.

12. **Conveniently "forget" your underwear while dressing for a social event.**
Make sure you tell him when you're almost there. One married mistress told me that when she and her husband arrived at a party one night, she told him she "accidentally" forgot her underwear. She said her husband hovered around

her that night, making sure no other man got too close. On the way home he was so turned on that they had to pull over and make love right there in the car!

13. **Take a shower together.**
Wash his back and he'll wash yours.

14. **Go out to dinner at a romantically secluded restaurant.**
If the restaurant has booths, request the waiter seat you in one, and sit together on one side of the booth. Have a nice leisurely dinner, and indulge in each other's company.

15. **Take him shopping with you to your favorite lingerie store. Buy an outfit he likes.**
Give his eyes a treat.

16. **When you get home, don't forget to wear it that evening.**
This reinforces that what he likes is important to you.

17. **Take him to the men's section and have him buy what you like.**
Give your eyes a treat.

18. **Tell him how sexy he looks when he wears it.**
That will encourage him to wear it again and again.

19. **Take a bubble-bath together.**
Rub a dub dub, live out a fantasy in your tub.

20. **Have a bouquet of balloons sent to his job to say I love you.**
This is a marvelous way to show your man how wonderful it feels to receive something special from a loved one. Many times men who don't send flowers simply don't realize the value they'll receive from doing this. Sometimes, we have to show them the way.

21. **Give him a love ticket that reads, "Tonight's the night."**
When he redeems his ticket, give him a night he'll remember forever.

22. **Prepare a candlelight dinner together.**
This is one of the most romantic ways to spend an evening at home together. Cooking together is sensual and fun.

23. **Have a romantic dinner catered in.**
This way you can enjoy your candlelight dinner without all the work.

24. **Give each other a sensuous oil massage.**
If it leads to a night of impassioned lovemaking, go with it and enjoy yourselves.

25. **Fix dinner in your apron (and nothing else).**
He'll know what's for dessert.

26. **Make up a sexual report card for him and give him an A+.**
Make sure he's making love to you the way you like it so you won't have to "cheat" on his report card.

27. **Read *The Sensuous Woman* by J.**
This book has timeless sensual power sure to enhance your intimate relationship.

28. **Practice some of the lessons in this classic love manual on your man.**
J's book is full of love exercises. Be sure to practice them on him.

29. **Tell him how good you feel when you're with him.**
That's a definite turn-on for him.

30. **Accept *any* gift he gives you with genuine enthusiasm.**
It really is the thought that counts.

31. **Greet him at the door on Halloween.**
After all the trick or treaters have gone to bed, greet him in a trench coat (nothing else), and flash him when he opens the door. Make sure you wait until you're sure it's him!

32. **Go for a romantic ride in your car.**
Find a secluded place, and make love in the back seat.

33. **Rent a hotel room, call him on the job, and tell him you're waiting for him in hotel room number ---.**
You're guaranteed to get a reaction from this one!

34. **Lather him up for his shave.**
Tell him how good his skin feels.

35. **Go for a wild, erotic limousine ride together.**
Make sure you tell the driver to put up the privacy shield.

36. **Take him shopping with you.**
Let him pick out an outfit he'd like to see you in.

37. **Go shopping with him.**
Now it's your turn to pick an outfit you want to see him in.

38. **Find out how many exciting places you can make love in your house besides the bedroom.**
This will be a most exciting treasure hunt.

39. **Slow dance together on your favorite song.**
Pick one you danced to when you were just getting to know each other.

40. **Go out to a night club and paint the town!**
Got any high heel sneakers?

41. **Go to a drive-in movie.**
Be sure to steam up those windows!

42. **Treat yourself to a day in a spa.**
Have a makeover, massage, pedicure, and manicure. A big part of keeping your love life exciting is taking the time to be good to yourself.

43. **Buy him tickets to his favorite sporting event.**

44. **Take a romantic stroll in the moonlight together.**
Gaze at the stars together and savor the romantic moment.

45. **Splurge and treat yourself to a new outfit.**
Remember--be good to yourself.

46. **Spend quiet time together just laying in each other's arms.**
No instruction needed.

47. **Rent an X-rated video, and watch it together.**
This can be a powerful aphrodisiac.

48. **Massage his neck after a hard day at the job.**
Another stress-buster.

49. **Let him massage your neck to relax you.**

50. **Have a lingerie fashion show.**
Send him an invitation that reads, *"For Your Eyes Only."*

51. **Give him a coupon redeemable for *One Forgiveness--No expiration date.***

52. **Send him a bellygram on his job. This surprise is perfect for a special occasion like his birthday. Hire a belly dancer to dance for him.**

53. **Take a second honeymoon.**
Go to an exotic place like Hawaii or the Bahamas.

54. **Take a boudoir photo setting.**
This one's a sure-fire eye-opener for him. Have a photo-album made of you draped in sexy lingerie. Many boudoir studios also do couple shoots. Take some sensual pictures together.

55. **Do a boudoir calendar.**

56. **When he leaves for work in the morning, compliment him now and then on how sexy he looks.**
Make sure he notices you noticing him.

57. **Take a luxurious and soothing bubble bath by yourself.**
This relieves tension and helps you relax.

58. **Do a strip-tease dance for him.**

59. **Have a sensual interlude in a swimming pool or hot tub.**

60. **Go on a lone shopping spree.**
Buy yourself something deliciously wicked.

61. **Let him make you *Queen For A Day*.**
Your wish is his command.

62. **Make him *King For A Day*.**
His wish is your command.

63. **Buy him a special present.**
Wrap it and leave it in his car so he'll find it before he drives off to work in the morning.

64. **Write him a love note.**
Leave it in his suit pocket. If he's going on an out-of-town business trip, leave him a sensual note in his luggage.

65. **Take time out to talk.**
Talk to each other every night.

66. **Buy yourself some new perfume, and put a little dab in all the right places.**
A recent study found that setting the sexual ambience to appeal to all the senses makes for good lovemaking. Perfume seductively arouses the sense of smell.

67. **Give him a *love prescription*.**
Make sure it reads: "No expiration date and unlimited refills."

68. **Get up early together to watch the beautifully vivid sunrise.**

69. **Mail him a love poem or love letter.**
One married mistress mailed her husband a sexy love letter while she was away visiting her parents. Her husband said he was so hot for her, he couldn't wait for her to get back. She was definitely the only "mistress" on his mind.

70. **Take a leisurely late night drive to a look-out point, and enjoy the sparkle of the city lights.**

71. **Go on a secluded picnic together.**
One married mistress says she and her husband make sure they go to a picnic area with a large picnic table, so they can make out in the wee hours of the night.

72. **Buy some sensual satin sheets to make love on.**
This one appeals to the sense of touch.

73. **Take a day off in the middle of the week, and spend it together.**
A mid-week surprise is always welcome.

74. **Tell him how happy you feel waking up knowing he's laying beside you every morning.**

75. **Make a private-label X-rated video together starring the two of you.**

Notice that weaved into the list are moments created for the sole purpose of being good to yourself. The more pleasurable moments you take the time to indulge in, the more relaxed you will be and ready to enjoy romantic moments with your love mate.

Let Me at Him!

The purpose of having a list of 75 activities is so you can have a wide variety at your disposal. That doesn't mean you have to act out each one. Do what your relationship will allow. Sometimes, when you take an enhancement seminar or read a book to improve your love life, it's easy to get carried away and try too many adventures too quickly. This can take your partner by surprise, and his reaction may not be as enthusiastic as you'd like. Most people don't like change, and many don't take to surprises. Be sure to take your other half's feelings into consideration, and test the waters slowly.

If you've prepared a hotly amorous evening and plan to "rock his world" when he gets home, make sure he's in the mood. His boss may have already rocked it in a negative way by giving him a hard time on his job. If it is evident he's had a bad day, postpone your plans for another time. Part of being a married mistress is taking stress out of your intimate environment--not adding to it by pressuring your partner into doing something he's not really in the mood for.

"May I Have a Rain Check, Please?"

One couple who engage in a passionate marital love affair say that when one of them is not in the mood for lovemaking, they can ask for a rain check. "It works in grocery stores," Marie points out. "Why can't it work at home?"

Marie says that John's firefighting job is physically tiring. She notes that sometimes when she's in the mood for a night of enjoyable lovemaking, she can tell as soon as he walks in the door he's "worn out."

John says if he is too tired and Marie has on her sexy lingerie, he always makes sure he tells her how sensational she looks, but then he politely explains he needs to rest and asks for a rain check.

"It works for me," affirms Marie. She admits there are some nights he's ready for love and she's not. In that case, she's the one to ask for a rain check.

It's a good idea to integrate a rain check system in your marital affair. As two different individuals, you and your partner aren't always on the same clock.

There will be times when you're in an amorous mood and he's not and vice versa. When that happens, be up front with one another. Rather than go through the motions and put up with having sex when you're not in the mood, ask for a rain check. Remember, good sex is all in your head. If you are fatigued, stressed, or preoccupied you won't enjoy the sexual adventure half as much. Romance works better when there are two willing entities.

Now I suggest Judy, our romance novel reader, put her romance novel down for a spell and create some fantasies of her own with her man--don't you agree? If she can't manage that, instead of scolding her husband for trying to romance her, her second alternative would be to sweetly ask him for a rain check.

Love Enhancer Exercise

Pick three items off the "75 Ways to Spice Up Your Love Life" list, and do them during the week.

My Romance Novel

In your Married Mistress Workbook (see page 15), please complete the following exercise:

Write a mini-romance novel. Re-create one of your favorite romantic fantasies starring you as the heroine and your mate as the man who romantically sweeps you away. Let your imagination take the story wherever you want to go. Be creative! Alter your physical appearance in the story if you like. For example, if you've always wanted to be taller, slimmer, shorter, or more voluptuous--*make it so!*

Twenty-Four

Recipes for Lovers

If you don't know quite where to begin your romance bonanza, don't despair. This chapter has an appetizing mix of recipes for lovers, giving you a range of amorous delights to choose from. As with any recipe, you may substitute any ingredients with ones more pleasing to your individual lifestyle.

These recipes were concocted and written by friends of the author and women who are indulging in marital affairs. They tested the recipes on their loved ones and guarantee them pleasing to your intimate palate.

Rejuvenator

1 exhausted body
1 relaxed body
2 cold, hard stiff glasses of water or lemonade
2 tablespoons of kisses
1 long, lustful hug with anxious arms
2 cups of nuts or chips

Wrap anxious arms tightly around lover's tired body for long, lustful hug. Sprinkle one tablespoon of kisses gently on mate's face. Guide tired body over to couch. Spoon out remaining tablespoon of sugar (kisses). Serve drinks and nuts or chips. Relax and enjoy.

Prepared in the kitchen of: Rose & Earl Smith

♥ ♥

Romance With A Lime Twist

1 large bathtub
3 large limes cut in quarters
3 drops of lime scented cologne
4 candles
1 bar of apple scented soap
1 bottle of massage oil in your favorite scent
(my favorite is vanilla)
linen sheet
1 lit fireplace
2 lovers

Fill bath with warm water, add limes and cologne. Light candles and place around tub, turn off lights. Carefully blend two lovers equipped with everything a body desires. Using the water as a flotation device, place lips together and kiss. Make sure to breathe properly, the steam can get pretty hot. Rub bodies with apple scented soap making sure to get every contour.

Go into room with fireplace. Laying on the sheet, blend two lovers with massage oil. Rub oiled bodies together making sure to arouse every inch. Place lips together and kiss, kiss, kiss. Romance with a lime twist is complete when both bodies have a golden warmth. Indulge in this dish any time of the day.

Prepared in the kitchen of Renee & Dennis Martinez

♥ ♥

Surprise Evening Out

1 baby sitter
A reservation for two at his favorite restaurant
1 surprise visit to mate's office
1 gorgeous red rose
2 dashes of sexy fragrance
1 delicious dress
1/2 ounce of lingerie
2 1/2 cups of cuddling
4 cups of good conversation
1 1/2 ounce of "sweet nothings"
1 bottle of good wine
Endless love

Mix arrangements for spouse's favorite restaurant with baby sitter and rose. Prepare yourself with fragrance and delicious dress. Set aside lingerie for later. With ingredients properly in place, make a surprise "appearance" to mate's office presenting him with one beautiful rose and "sweet nothings" in his ear. Put aside some "sweet nothings" for later.

Whisk mate to favorite restaurant and enjoy seductive dinner by candlelight. Add good wine, conversation, and throw in cuddling. Sprinkle more "sweet nothings" in lover's ear throughout the evening. Return home and top with 1/2 ounce of sensual lingerie when appropriate. Mate should be thoroughly heated by now. Enjoy the company of your lifetime partner with endless love.

Prepared in the kitchen of: Patti & John Tatman

♥ ♥

Treasure Hunt

1 gift (picked with your lover in mind)
gift wrap
2 glasses of something cold to drink
1 bubble bath
3 or 4 pieces of perfumed stationery
1 pen
1 soft bath towel
1 bathing beauty
1 eager partner
1 ounce of his and her underwear
A pinch of sexy fragrance

Take one gift and wrap with tender loving care. Gently place in center of dining room table. Using pen and perfumed stationery, lovingly write the following notes to your lover:

1. *For you, with love.* (Place note on top of gift.)
2. *Come into the bedroom; something's waiting for you on the bed.* (Place this one up under the gift so he'll read it when he picks the gift up.)
3. *Remove every stitch of your clothing, and come into the bathroom. Be sure to wrap this towel around your sexy bottom.* (Place this note on the bed next to the towel.)
4. *I want you.* (Tack this one onto the mirror in the bathroom.)

Take the cold drinks and place them on a tray in your bedroom. Run a warm, relaxing bubble bath. Undress and soothe your body in the tub. Sprinkle the water with a pinch of fragrance. Await your lover's arrival. After your bath together, dry each other off, and watch each other dress in the sexy underwear. Enjoy your drinks in the bedroom and whatever comes next.

Prepared in the kitchen of: Shirley & Vincent Pugh

♥ ♥

Kisses In The Moonlight

1 moonlit beach (or moonlit evening)
2 loving bodies
A touch of hand-holding
A pinch of hugging
Lots of kisses
2 cups of passion
2 softly lit candles
2 delicious drinks of choice
1 bowl of Hershey's® chocolate kisses

Take a long stroll on a moonlit beach (or sidewalk in your neighborhood) while holding hands. Make sure to stir in a pinch of hugs with a cup of kisses to sweeten the evening. If on the beach, remove your shoes, and step into ankle-deep water. Slowly add two cups of passion. As the evening becomes too cool, head home for a romantic nite cap for two including two softly lit candles and a bowl of chocolate kisses.

Prepared in the kitchen of Shirley & Vincent Pugh

♥ ♥

The Bridal Basket

1 medium straw basket with handle
1 bottle of scented bubble bath
A handful of bath beads (preferably in the bride's wedding colors)
1 bar of scented soap
2 champagne glasses
1 bottle of champagne
3 scented candles
1 cup of confetti or glitter
clear Saran Wrap
1 bow

Place each item in basket except Saran Wrap and bow. When you have items attractively arranged, spread the confetti or glitter on top. Wrap with Saran Wrap and add bow. Attach a love recipe to basket to help the bride and groom start their marriage on a very passionate note.

From the kitchen of Renee Martinez

♥ ♥

A Special Celebration

4-6 candles
1 ounce pina colada love-oil
1 bottle of scented body lotion
2 partying bodies
1 reason to celebrate (or several or *make up one!*)
5 tapes of love music (Luther Vandross)
1 bottle of non-alcoholic champagne
All the time in the world

Set the scene before the "celebrated party" arrives. Light the candles, chill the champagne, and put in a sexy Luther Vandross tape. Put lotion and love-oil aside for later use. When party arrives, begin celebration with a full body massage, and let the magic unfold. *Repeat as needed!*

Prepared in the kitchen of Darlene Smart

♥ ♥

The Massage

4 tablespoons soft music
1 dash of candlelight
1 sprinkle of fragrance
1/2 ounce of lingerie
2 seasoned lovers
1/2 cup of cuddling
2 cups caressing
Satin sheets
1 breakfast in bed
1/4 cup fantasy fulfilled

Light candles, and put on soft music. Prepare lover with one fifteen minute massage, kneading, wrapping and stirring. Complete by mixing on soft satin sheets, kissing, caressing and cuddling till done. Layer with "love." Top with one breakfast in bed. Indulge as often as time and calories permit.

Prepared in the kitchen of: Catherine & William Nixon

♥ ♥

Ride 'Em Cowboy

2 cowboy hats
2 pair of cowboy boots
1 willing cowboy
1 sexy cowgirl
1 well-worn pair of jeans (cut into shorts)
1 garter belt
1 pair of silky stockings
1 sexy, black or red bra
1 pair of men's underwear
2-4 candles
Slow music of choice

Put on hat, bra, jean-shorts, stockings, garter belt, and boots. When your "cowboy" arrives, hand him his outfit and instruct him to "saddle-up." Light candles and play music. Tell your beau he is your "stud of choice," and his goal in your "rodeo" is to see how long he can ride. Keep track of the winning time. *Yippie Keye Yay Keye Yo!*

Marie Zehrung and John Standefer

♥ ♥

Twenty-Five

Do You Think You're Sexy?

Attitude Is Everything

Feeling sexy *is* sexy. "It has everything to do with your attitude," says fashion and image consultant, Nancy Fisher. She affirms that even when a woman is wearing a sensual garment underneath straight-laced business attire, if she feels sexy she will exude an added air of confidence.

Is the Other Woman Sexy?

Fisher contends that the reason the other woman often seems to have the upper hand is because of her self-confidence. She says the other woman is extremely convincing at carrying off an attitude of sexual assuredness. More than one married man interviewed admitted their paramours attracted them because of a sexy attitude. As one man put it, "Sherri is so sexy to me, and not because she's a perfect size five. She's what most people consider overweight, but to me she's beautiful. All I see when I look at her is a woman who *feels sexy*. Nothing is more erotic than that." Fisher agrees. "Your sensuality has nothing to do with your dress size--attitude is everything."

If you think you're sexy, you are. In contrast, if you feel self-conscious in lingerie while you're trying to turn your man on, your insecurity will be as boldly stated as a run in your stocking. The negative vibes of your body language will override the message you're sending that you want to enjoy a night of lovemaking. The results will be embarrassing for both of you.

Your Sensual Best

How can you become more sensual? The first item on your agenda is not to go out and buy something wicked to make his mouth water; that's second. The first and most potent ingredient you need in your sensual makeup is the right demeanor. Using your *Married Mistress Workbook (see page 15),* answer the following questions yes or no:

1. When wearing a short dress, are you constantly tugging at it, trying to conceal your thighs?

2. Do you wear dresses whose hemlines fall below the knee because you think your knees are too fat?

3. Do you avoid bikini underwear because of a heavy bottom or heavy hips?

4. Do you feel sexy in lingerie?

5. Are you more comfortable making love with the lights off?

6. Do you avoid lingerie because instead of seeing a sensual woman you see a woman with various figure flaws? (Small breasts, sagging breasts, heavy hips or thighs, etc.)

Pay attention to your emotional attitude because a healthy attitude is the most essential ingredient in your sensual makeup. If you feel the need to cover up, it's not your body that needs the immediate change, it's your attitude.

Twenty-Six

Watch Those Curves

A big part of being at your sensual best is feeling good about your body. It's hard to want to reveal yourself in sexy lingerie if you're concerned about being overweight. Fisher says women who are overweight often dress fat. They try to cover their bodies and hide their figure flaws. She calls the tent look "disastrous" for full-figured women because while it may hide flaws, it also hides attributes like curvy hips, a small waist, and a shapely bustline. Frequently, a full-figured woman's desire to dress fat spills over into her bedtime dress.

Dr. Barbara De Angelis observes that a woman's need to cover up because of her self-consciousness about her flaws, often conflicts with her man's need to look at her. In her magazine article, "Why Black Lace Turns Him On," De Angelis says that a woman probably notices her figure flaws more than her man does. She says that while the woman is thinking, "Cover up, cover up," her man is thinking, "Reveal, reveal."

Sondra, who attended the Married Mistress Seminar, believes men and women do what she calls *selective seeing:* "Most of the time I just cringe when Nick sees me naked, or in lingerie. All I can think about are my sagging breasts, bulging tummy, and cellulite. But he seems to love my body. Maybe all women feel badly about their bodies in some respect. I think when Nick looks at me, he focuses on what he likes and blocks out the rest, just as when I look at my body I focus on what I don't like and block out the rest."

It's interesting to note that many men are tired of the Madison Avenue version of skin and bones. Most men like curvaceous women. Think of our sex symbols: Marilyn Monroe, Lillian Russell, and Mae West. These women were all full-figured beauties. And you didn't see them hiding their figure under an over abundance of material. Writer and talk show host, Bob Berkowitz, says the media has sold women "a bill of goods." He confirms that the anorexic look turns most men off. So don't hide your curves--flaunt them. If your weight doesn't cause you medical problems, don't worry about reducing yourself to an unbecoming shapeless frame. Instead, concern yourself with making what you have look smashing.

Diet *Is* a Four-Letter Word

Diets don't work. We've heard it again and again, yet our thin obsessed society still spends billions yearly trying to diet, hoping to lose weight. In his book, *Fit or Fat,* Covert Bailey discusses our view of thin and how much better it is for people, unhappy with their bodies, to tighten up and tone what they have rather than trying to fit into a size five and look like an unhealthy skeleton.

Kim White, a physical fitness trainer, says to remember when toning and tightening, think of an iceberg. The thinnest part will see results first. She suggests focusing your ambition on tightening and firming the muscle. White prepared the following body fat chart filled with tips to help women achieve a healthy, taut body-frame:

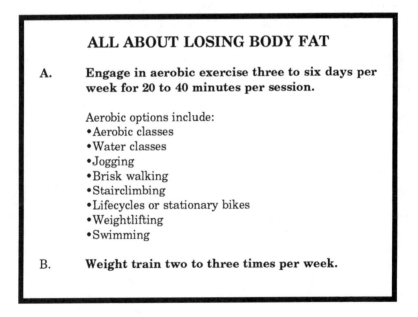

ALL ABOUT LOSING BODY FAT

A. **Engage in aerobic exercise three to six days per week for 20 to 40 minutes per session.**

Aerobic options include:
- Aerobic classes
- Water classes
- Jogging
- Brisk walking
- Stairclimbing
- Lifecycles or stationary bikes
- Weightlifting
- Swimming

B. **Weight train two to three times per week.**

C.   Improve Your Eating Habits.

♦ Eat regularly. At *least* three times per day. Going for hours without eating will actually encourage your body to store fat. Eating small meals regularly will allow the body to burn a higher percentage of calories from fat.

♦ Monitor your fat grams. Carbohydrate and protein calories are burned more readily than fat calories. Carbohydrates and proteins have 4 calories per gram. Fats have 9 calories per gram. Limit your fat grams to 20% or less of your total daily caloric intake.

Example: 20% of 1500* calories = 300 fat calories. 300 divided by 9 = 33 fat grams per day.

*Note: 1500 calories may be inappropriate for your age, metabolic needs, and current level of fitness. See a registered dietician or your physician to determine your appropriate caloric needs.

D.   Monitor Your Calories.

If a decrease in body fat does not occur by doing all of the above, then begin monitoring your total caloric intake. Even a very low fat eating program will not result in fat loss if total calories are excessive. Carbohydrates and proteins will be stored as fat if the total calories are excessive or inadequate. Note: The average fat percentage loss is .5% per month.

Start where you are today. Feel good about your body, and show off your curves--don't hide them. By being comfortable about your body and who you are, you'll present an aura of sexuality and femininity. Being in that sensual frame of mind allows you to feel comfortable revealing seductive lingerie sure to set your man on fire.

Twenty-Seven

Silk Undies & Lace Teddies

Why Men Love Lingerie

Lacy, racy underdress has been turning men on since long before the 1800's. According to Christina Probert, author of *Lingerie In Vogue,* oodles of seductive, soft material have always played a practical as well as aesthetic role in every woman's wardrobe.

There's something about the femininity and sensual beauty of tender lace and the soft feel of silk that sends most men into an erotic frenzy. The other woman's sexy undergarments beckon men to wade deep into the waters of infidelity, asking them to risk it all. As a married mistress, you can offer your man that same type of lure without any risk. Lingerie helps you set the mood for dynamite sex.

The Lady in Lace

Never underestimate the power of titillating lingerie. One of the popular television talk shows recently highlighted the goings-on between a prostitute and her clients. During the show, a middle-aged prostitute, dolled up with heavy makeup and brassy blonde hair, shared her experiences. Surprisingly, she confessed that she seldom engaged in sexual intercourse with many of her clients. She made $45.00 to $50.00 an hour doing something much more shocking. It was surprising a woman could actually make her living this way. She earned her keep by modeling lingerie husbands and boyfriends originally bought for their wives or girlfriends. She said that when their women politely (or impolitely) refuse to wear the sensual gifts, the men become her clients, paying her $45.00 and sometimes $50.00

an hour to wear the lingerie their partners refuse to wear. She said sometimes sex occurred, but most of the time the men just watched her model the seductive outfits for them. This example goes a long way in showing just how important setting a seductive atmosphere is for many men. And some men, unfortunately, will seek that atmosphere elsewhere if their partners fail to provide it.

Sexy Undergarments Aren't Just for You

Just as men like the right atmosphere set for good sex, so do women. Women also get turned on looking at certain body parts of the male anatomy enhanced by sexy underwear. Don't get into the habit of being the only one donning sexy underdress. Encourage your man to show off his body, too. Buy him sexy undies you'd like to see him sport. This serves a two-fold purpose. First, it helps make setting the sexual atmosphere a common goal. A marital affair won't go far unless both parties share in creating the excitement. Second, it makes both of you more comfortable. If you're the only one wearing sexy undergarments, you may eventually feel like you're the only one concerned about turning him on. This can cause a woman to wonder if her man is interested in giving her mutual satisfaction. When both of you share the scene, you can arouse each other and take an equal part in setting the mood.

Dress for Sexcess

As in everyday dress, you want to wear lingerie that flatters your figure. The more you know about your body and what type of clothing shows off your attributes, the easier it is for you to look your best.

Buying lingerie is no different than selecting outerwear. The more you know about different types of lingerie, the easier it will be to pick out the type you will look and feel your best in. It can be said feeling comfortable is even more important when selecting undergarb because you're exposing more of yourself. In this section, we'll cover (or uncover) two areas. First, lingerie boutique owner Martha Doster will discuss different types of sensual dress. Doster, owner of Body Bueno, has been in the retail lingerie business for over fifteen years. Second, at the end of this section, you'll have a listing of body types at your fingertips as well as what type of lingerie looks best on specific body silhouettes.

According to Doster, the one piece of lingerie most of her male customers rave about is the sexy bustier. The bustier is a waist-length, tight fitting, often strapless garment, with or without garters attached. It's similar to the old fashioned corset women used to painfully squeeze their bodies into to give the appearance of a slimmer waistline.

What makes a bustier more comfortable than the corset, explains Doster, is the wonder material called Lycra, the trademark name for a spandex fabric used in much of today's fashionable underwear and swimwear. Doster says Lycra is ideal for all figure types. "It pulls in and tightens everything." The most flattering type of bustier for a full-hipped woman, or a woman with a tummy bulge, is one called a "merry widow." This version is longer than the waist-length bustier. It falls over the hip area pulling everything into a seductive, slimming fit.

When looking for sexy undies, she suggests most women, especially if their bottom or thighs are full, look for the high cut versions. "The higher cut gives a longer, slimmer leg," explains Doster. She advises avoiding bikini underwear if you're bottom heavy. A full brief with a high cut leg, made with Lycra material is more flattering.

G-strings enhance as long as your bottom isn't too full or too flat. G-strings tend to make flat bottoms look even flatter which make them look droopy. Lycra also helps lift a drooping rear. Since G-strings can be uncomfortable, Doster suggests trying a version of a G-string called the thong. It offers a more comfortable fit because it has more material than the G-string, resulting in a wider piece of elastic in the back.

If you have large breasts, Doster suggests wearing stretch lace lingerie or lingerie made with Lycra. There are gowns available that offer more bust support than others. Women with small breasts can wear push-up bras (they typically come with removable padding) or sexy shelf bras which have underwire without the cup. An underwire bra also gives a small-breasted woman a fuller look. Doster advises women to be open to trying the new underwire bras. "Most women are under the notion that underwire bras are uncomfortable. They're made much better now, and there are many comfortable ones on the market today."

Doster says the most common mistake women make when purchasing lingerie is having a preconceived notion of what will look good on them. "Too many times the image they have of what looks good is from a fashion magazine where the model's shape is different from their shape." When shopping for lingerie she advises, instead of going with what looks good on a model, look for pieces that have slenderizing, vertical lines. She also says knowing your body and dressing for your body type is the best way to avoid making the mistake of buying something unflattering to your figure. There are four common silhouettes. Read over the four types and determine which one fits you best. Then use the "Look For Lingerie With" section as a guide when selecting sexy undergarments.

Body Types

Body Type 1	*Body Type 2*
Even proportions, hourglass curves, definite waist even with weight gain. Gains weight around the waist, thighs, stomach and rear.	Pear-shaped proportions, can be 2 sizes smaller on top than on bottom. Gains weight in outer thighs and rear.
Look For Lingerie With:	Look For Lingerie With:
•Good bust support. •High cut legs. •Two-piece garments with waist-high bottoms. •Vertical or diagonal lines.	•Ruffles or a draped bust. •Padded or underwire bra. •Shelf bra. •Short skirts that offer good rear and thigh coverage. •Two-piece garments with tap pant bottoms. •Wide-set straps to visually widen chest and shoulders.
Avoid:	Avoid:
•Strapless garments without underwire. •Low-cut legs. (They shorten the silhouette.) •Garments that expose the tummy (if you have a tummy bulge.)	•Low-cut legs which emphasize heavy hips and thighs. •V-neck styles.

Body Type 3	*Body Type 4*
Shoulders are broader than hips, rear is flat. Gains weight in breasts, midriff and stomach. Look for lingerie with: •Good bust support. •High-cut legs. •Two-piece garments with waist-high bottoms. •Blouson styles to camouflage a tummy bulge. Avoid: •Skirted pieces. •Ruffles at the bust. •Strapless garments without underwire.	Weight is evenly distributed, has few curves. Gains weight over entire body. Look for lingerie with: •Material darker at the waistline or wrapped panels that visually slim the waist. •Material that gathers at the bust. •Underwiring in the garment to add more shape and support. •Sweetheart necklines which visually enlarge the bust. Avoid: •Skimpy pieces or bikinis which emphasize lack of curves. •Boxy tank tops. •A garment with vertical patterns.

Going Undercover

A lively way to experiment with sensual lingerie in the privacy of your home is to have a lingerie party or fashion show. Many lingerie shops will come to your house and showcase their alluring "wears" for you and a few friends. Some lingerie companies exclusively market their fashions through home parties.

One of the largest home party outfits is UndercoverWear. The company was founded based on the 007 Bond theme. Each representative who joins UndercoverWear becomes an UndercoverWear "Agent" and is assigned an "Agent number."

Connie Minard, who's been an UndercoverWear Agent for almost ten years says the home parties, which UndercoverWear dubs "lingerie fashion shows," are a fun and unique way for women to shop for sensual lingerie. She says the goal of the fashion shows is for the guests to enjoy an evening filled with *fun, fashion, and fantasy.*

UndercoverWear suggests a mood and feeling with every item they sell. Names like "Sweet Seduction," "His Fantasy," "Captivating

You," "Not Tonight I Have A Headache," "Ladies Night Out Cami," and "An Affair To Remember," tell the story.

An interesting icebreaker and trademark of UndercoverWear is their Sexuality Test which allows each guest to test their sensuality by asking questions like:

1.   If you feel women should enjoy sex as much as men....20 points

2.   If you've read any literature within the last six months on how to improve your lovemaking...15 points

3.   If he has ever said, "No, please try it this way," and you did...20 points.

4.   If he cries openly, do you:
        • Love him more...20 points
        • Think he's a wimp...-20 points

5.   During your most intimate moment, he says, "Honey, describe me." Would you describe him as:
        • Pee Wee Herman...-5 points
        • Tom Thumb...10 points
        • Big Ben...20 points

For more information about how you can experience a lingerie show in your home call your local lingerie store or you can call UndercoverWear at 617-938-0007.

Another way to experiment with different looks in lingerie is to browse through some of the many lingerie catalogues. Even if you buy most of your undergarb locally the catalogues will spark your imagination, helping you put together some stunning outfits. You can call to request a catalogue from Victoria's Secret at 800-888-8200, or call Frederick's of Hollywood to obtain their catalogue at 800-323-9525. You can also send $2.00 (refunded with first order) to "Lady Annabelle Sensual Lingerie for the Rubenesque Woman" to Evelyn Rainbird, PO Box 6500, Englewood, NJ 07631.

One fun activity for you and your mate is to go through the catalogue together. Even if you don't buy anything, shopping for lingerie together is a sensual activity.

Scentsational

Sweet, sensual smells and silky lingerie go hand-in-hand. Seductive scents are like ice cream--there are so many tempting flavors to choose from. Perfume helps set an inviting ambience.

Here are some interesting things you can do with scents:
1. Dab a little on a cotton ball, and place the ball in your lingerie drawer.

2. Rub a tiny bit of cologne on a light bulb to scent the room.

3. Put some in all the "strategic points" of your body (in other words, the areas he'll be exploring).

4. Put a little in your bath water.

5. Spray some on your stocking feet, the scent will drift upward.

6. Lightly spray the pillowcases.

7. Spray cologne on your comb before combing your hair.

As with ice cream, savor the flavor, but don't overdo. Only use one or two of these items at a time.

Part IV
Your Positive
Mental Attitude

Twenty-Eight

I'll Be Good to Me

Time Out

It's finally five o'clock. You thought the work day would go on forever. Your boss was on your back all day, and all the customers did was complain. This has been a long, stress-filled day. You gather up your briefcase and race to your car--keys in hand. You can't wait to get home to rest your tired bones. All you can think of is a nice, relaxing evening to recuperate from your work day.

You grab the mail out of the mailbox while anxiously turning the key in the front door of your safe haven. All you want to do is change into your comfortable jeans and relax for awhile. "Mom, look!" Your daughter runs up to you excitedly. "Guess what happened to me today!" She goes on about her day. "Mom, can you give me a ride to Marsha's?" your son hollers down the hall as soon as he hears your footsteps. As you quickly struggle to shift gears in midstream, you begin to think you're just starting your second work-shift--*Time out.*

You don't have to shift gears right away. One of the most important things we can teach our children and ourselves is that we all need quiet time. "All I want to do when I get home is just unwind for a few minutes before I start playing Mom," says Kathleen, a married mistress, who works all day as a secretary.

One of Janet Jackson's biggest hits in the 1980's helped women ask their lovers, *"What have you done for me lately?"* I'd like to turn the tables and ask, what have you done for yourself lately? Many women with jam-packed schedules face the problem of making time for themselves. It's fine to work at improving your intimate relationship and your role as wife and mother, but it's also primary to remember your special needs.

Today's working woman leads a busy life. If you're a homemaker and have children, you have one job. If you have children and work outside the home, you easily have two full-time jobs. It's easy to get caught up in your hectic daily routine and forget about yourself in the process. This chapter addresses the importance of being good to yourself.

Carol Rohlfing, *Family Circle's* health editor, reports that the newest research indicates an overload of "silent" stressors plague most women today. Rohlfing says one of these stressors for many women is not having any quiet time reserved. She emphasizes that "silent" stressors may be just as harmful to your physical and emotional well-being and health as major stressors like loss of a job or moving. A steady diet of "silent" stressors can suppress your immune system and cause you to be sick more often.

Out of 35,000 *Family Circle* readers who responded to their survey about how the readers spend their time, 19% admitted they were dissatisfied with their time alone, while 20% had no time alone at all. When asked if their lack of private time affected their sex lives, 42% of the women admitted their sex lives were "sometimes affected." Another one third admitted their sex lives were "often affected."

Don't Give All Your Gold Away

A solid marital relationship fashions itself around the saying: give gold, get gold. The more you give to your intimate relationship, the more you get back. But one mistake you do not want to make is giving all your gold away, not leaving any for yourself. If Ed McMahon rang the doorbell and handed you a check for ten thousand dollars, you'd probably be ecstatic. However, if you systematically gave every bit of that money to loved ones and others around you without leaving any for yourself, you might be a little resentful of those who took, thinking only of themselves. You'd also probably be a little angry at yourself for giving too much. Well, that's what many women do with their time. They give so much away, they forget to reserve some for themselves.

A woman today can easily allow commitments to pull her in too many directions. Demands of work, household chores, children, and spousal needs can send a woman into a never ending spiral of doing everything to please others around her while leaving little energy to take care of herself. If you don't see to your needs, who will?

On the day you have to drive your daughter to her girl scout meeting, you're not feeling well. Do you think she'll come into your room and say, "Gee mom, you look awful. Don't worry about taking me to girl scouts. I can go next week." Or, do you think she would rather you pick yourself up and carry your vomit bag with you in case you need it en route?

Can you see your son happily postponing part of his allowance for a week so you can buy those shoes you've been eyeing that have finally gone on sale for half price? Or, can you see him saying something more like, "But Mom! I promised Cheryl I'd take her to the movies this weekend! Anyway, you've got shoes!"

And what about your boss? Will he recognize that you need an afternoon off because of stress after working overtime two weeks straight? Can you hear him telling you: "I want you to get off that computer right now, and take the afternoon off. Grab your coat and purse, rush right home, and take a load off. I can tell you need a break." If you wait for other people to sense you need a break, you'll be in for a long wait.

Others around you won't be too anxious to forego their needs. Nevertheless, you know when you've had enough of taking care of everyone else. You know when you're too sick to chauffeur your daughter to her meeting. You know when you need to treat yourself to a new pair of shoes. And, you can sense when you need a break from on-the-job tension.

More women need to learn to include the word **_NO_** in their vocabularies because many have learned to take care of the world around them. That's fine, as long as they have limits and remember to take generous care of themselves.

As a woman, you must learn to treat yourself as well as you treat others around you. Sharon Anthony Bower and Gordon H. Bower, authors of *Asserting Yourself,* say that an assertive person can learn to negotiate mutually satisfactory resolutions to many situations. That means when you learn to assert yourself and make sure your needs are being met, the other person or people involved do not automatically lose out. You can often meet your needs as well as theirs. The Bowers caution that you may have trouble handling certain situations if you're in the habit of foregoing your needs for others. They maintain that your goal is to change the way you and others around you interact so *both* parties derive more satisfaction.

Feeling Good About Feeling Good

A major emotion most women must tackle to get to the business of enjoying private time is *GUILT*. In the magazine article, "Too Close For Comfort?" Sharon Johnson notes that most women are taught from childhood that a good wife and mother spends her time on her husband and children.

Many women don't allot time for themselves. Working women face a double dilemma--they feel guilty about working and having to be away from their children all day, so when they want some time alone, they feel they're robbing their families even more.

Ironically, by denying themselves vital private time to re-vitalize their energies, the very relationships women think they are helping, can easily end up in jeopardy. If a woman neglects her needs and drains herself to be there for others, her strain and stress will eventually wear on these relationships. She may even find herself snapping the heads off the loved ones she feels so obligated to make happy. In the book *Women's Burnout*, Dr. Herbert J. Freudenberger and Gail North call daily stress a "major aspect of a woman's burnout." They affirm that over a short period of time, an overload of stress produces a cranky, irritable person.

Just as a car cannot run without a charged battery, a woman must charge her emotional battery, or she will eventually run out of juice. Marlys Harris suggests you say the "Five Words That Will Make You Happier" aloud: *"I'm taking time for myself!"* While she acknowledges that it may seem self-indulgent for some women who want time alone, she emphasizes that every woman needs this special time at some point during her day. Resolve in your mind that this time will benefit the family you care about. Your embedded guilt may haunt you for awhile, but continue taking time, even if it's only 15 minutes to read a magazine article or just sit down and relax. You need time to unwind.

When you grant yourself time to re-energize your emotional battery, you'll be able to give more of your *loving self* to others, because you won't be suffering from emotional burnout.

Discovering You

It can be scary, especially for women who suffer from low self-esteem because they often feel more important through taking care of others. Taking care of self is hard for a woman who puts other people's needs first, or for a woman with low self-esteem because she believes she's not worth it.

If you've wrapped yourself up in other's needs, discovering you and fulfilling your needs may be a little intimidating at first. Give yourself time to adapt. The change may not happen overnight. Old beliefs and habits are like well-rooted weeds; these habits can be so deeply embedded, they become hard to pull up and get rid of. And just when you think you've gotten rid of all the weeds, you see another one take root to choke your progress.

If you're in the habit of living for others, your trip to self-discovery may be slow. Don't rush--take your time. When the weeds of your old habits and beliefs try to take hold, remind yourself that, like your husband and children, you are a *VIP--a Very Important Person*. Remember to shower yourself with the same measures of kindness and love you pour onto your family and friends. As a VIP-- *you're worth every ounce.*

Being Good to You Exercise

Now that you've resolved to give yourself the gift of time, what will you do with it? The main thing to remember is whatever you decide to do, make sure it offers relaxation and enjoyment for you.

There are a variety of things you can indulge in for a special treat. One of my clients makes January her extra special month. Cindy treats herself special throughout the year, and she uses the entire month of January to double her pleasures. "I indulge in spa treatments, make-overs, new clothes, quiet time retreats--anything that makes me feel good," says Cindy. It doesn't matter how much time you reserve as long as it's on a regular basis, or what you decide to engage in, as long as it makes you feel good.
Put aside time to do things like:

- ♥ Indulge in your favorite hobby,
- ♥ Exercise,
- ♥ Read a book,
- ♥ Treat yourself to a massage,
- ♥ Have a manicure or pedicure,
- ♥ Get a make-over,
- ♥ Go window shopping.

Working in your *Married Mistress Workbook (see page 15),* add to this list. Write down things you enjoy doing. Remember, one of the things many men find enticing about the other woman is that she takes care of herself. By taking the time to take care of your needs, you'll rejuvenate yourself and reward others around you by being more relaxed and not overworked.

Twenty-Nine

Mate Versus Mistress

Jake comes home after a stress-filled day at work and unloads on his wife. "I hate my job! Sometimes I wish I could pack it all in and go lay on a beach in the Bahamas for the rest of my natural life!"

He feels the scorpion-like sting of his wife's caustic reaction. "There you go again complaining about your job. Have you thought about what quitting would do to me and the kids? How would we eat? Where would we live? You know you can't quit your job!" She continues her tirade, reminding him of his many responsibilities. Jake immediately feels trapped and overburdened. He leaves his mate in the living room so he can flee from the anxiety she added to his day. After dinner, he makes his escape to the understanding arms of his carefree lover. The other woman is waiting for Jake with a warm reception. She immediately consoles him and allows him to express himself freely. She hugs him while telling him she understands his plight. She admits she shares his same frustration on her job from time to time. She comforts him. He feels relieved, freer. He can face his next day at work. She helped him get over his stress by not adding to it. Jake's intimate bond with the other woman deepens.

The Mate Mind-Set

While interviewing for this book, most of the men involved in extramarital affairs stated that one of the major elements they sought in an extramarital affair was freedom. To many of them, their mates represent a sense of responsibility. Some of them felt this obligation was overburdening at times. When asked what their relationships with their mates remind them of, these phrases kept cropping up:

- Providing shelter
- Keeping food on the table
- Taking care of the family
- Saving for retirement
- Paying for the mortgage (or rent)

These men were clearly seeing their marriages as knee-deep in responsibility. Unfortunately, some wives are there to serve as constant reminders of their seemingly overburdened load. When Jake's other half reminded him of his marital obligations, she was in what I refer to as the "mate mind-set." Her pessimistic frame of mind prevented her from giving Jake the understanding ear he needed.

While researching material for this book, I came across an eye-catching illustration. The back cover of the book, *Dave Barry's Guide To Marriage And Sex*, shows an illustration of two hands, one male, one female, joined together by matrimony--*and handcuffs!* That illustration directly drives home the point about the negative aspects of the mate frame of mind.

Marriages concrete in an overwhelming sense of obligation rather than love are ripe for extramarital interference. One of the biggest enticements the extramarital affair holds for both a married or attached man and his other woman is that they are together because of *want rather than need*.

When a married man justifiably or unjustifiably correlates marriage with hand-cuffs shackling him to his wife and all the marital responsibilities she drags along with her, the freedom of an extramarital affair is often irresistible. A woman who finds herself saying things like the following when reasoning with her spouse may be helping her mate to see their marriage in an unappealing light:

- Because you owe me.
- You're not going because you're married now--act like it.
- You should have gotten that out of your system before you married me.
- You made a commitment to us, we should be more important to you.

She may be adding to her mate's feeling that walking down the aisle replaces love and lust with responsibility and duty. That mistake can lead many married men down a vulnerable path, leading straight to the other woman's doorstep.

Mistress Mind-Set

Being in the mistress frame of mind as opposed to the mate's is like seeing your glass half full rather than half empty. The mistress mind-set accentuates the optimistic viewpoint rather than the pessimistic one.

In the magazine article, "Be An Optimist In Two Weeks," Dr. Martin Seligman defines the difference between optimism and pessimism: "The pessimist believes that bad things are permanent, pervasive, and unchangeable. The optimist, by contrast, believes that bad things are temporary, specific, and changeable."

Let's examine the difference in atmosphere when Jake made his escape to his mistress. When she opens the door to greet him, she acts as if she doesn't have a care in the world. He can come to her with his nagging problems, and she'll listen with concern. Since she knows that they cannot be together as often as they want, she's available whenever he needs her. This relaxed, empathetic atmosphere makes Jake's hunger for the affair grow. She doesn't bring the stress of her day to the hotel room with her. Her time with him is precious, so she makes the most of it.

He doesn't have a care in the world when he's with her. No mortgage, no children interrupting their time together, unadulterated freedom. Freedom from responsibility, and freedom from stress. That's what Jake's other woman represents to him.

Jake relishes his unstressed environment, especially after dealing with his wife's cruel criticisms. Her pessimistic view of his expression of job frustration pushed her further away from her husband. It was only when the other woman put the situation in an optimistic light for Jake by saying *I understand,* that he was able to unwind.

Understanding Wives

By empathizing with your partner when he is experiencing a difficult situation, you can easily adopt the positive side of the mistress's attitude.

One reason it was so much easier for Jake's mistress to be more understanding than his wife is because she is further removed from the situation than Jake's wife. Her finances are not linked with his.

Sometimes, when a person has a lot to lose in a given situation, it's difficult for them to remain rational. Jake's wife immediately correlated his job woes as "no food on the table." Often, when a person feels threatened or helpless in a situation, it's not unusual for them to strike out.

Employing a positive attitude sometimes requires removing yourself from the situation. It calls for replacing fear with feelings of empathy.

When Jake said he wished he could quit his job, was he telling his wife he was definitely quitting? No--he was merely venting his frustration. Haven't you ever felt like quitting your job? You know you have bills to pay, you're aware of your many responsibilities, but the situation at work is sometimes so frustrating, you wish you could leave it all behind. *Wish* is the operative word here. We all like to escape from the pressure cooker world of work now and then. If working forty to sixty hours a week was so pleasant, state lotteries would not be nearly as lucrative as they are. We all wish that sometimes we didn't have to work, but that doesn't mean we're going to pack it all in. When Jake said he would like to quit, he wasn't saying he was going to quit.

When his wife dutifully reminded him of his obligations, she only added to his tension. Now, if he had come home and announced that he was definitely going to quit, she would have been right to question his decision in a rational fashion. Jake's wife needed to realize that he was simply expressing a fantasy many frustrated nine-to-fivers share. By temporarily using the mistress mind-set, and removing herself from the situation, she will find it easier to empathize and say, "I understand." Then she will be the one growing closer to her husband, not the other woman.

Great Expectations

Some mates have high expectations of their love partners. Instead of wanting their partners to act as separate individuals, they want them to put the relationship and their needs first. As workshop leader Ellen Sue Stern notes in her magazine article "Too Many Expectations," this overwhelming attitude can strain the relationship.

"Projecting our expectations without considering what he wants, needs, or is capable of giving is a guaranteed recipe for disappointment," emphasizes Stern. She goes on to emphasize even though you may be close as a couple, you are two separate beings with individualized needs and wants.

Stern says the key to letting go of our over expectations is not to become perfectly loving at all times, putting your needs completely aside--but to have the ability to negotiate with your mate. That's where employing both mate and mistress traits can work to benefit your intimate relationship.

When the Mistress Becomes the Mate

There are times when you must adopt the rationale of the responsible mate. The goal is to call on both perspectives. Neither is all good or all bad. Both have certain characteristics that fit certain instances.

The other woman is not immune to possessing negative aspects of the mate frame of mind. One man claimed it was his mistresses' changed behavior that led him to end their fiery relationship. He said that when he started dating her, she was loads of fun. After awhile, she began pressuring him to tell his wife about them, and telling him how much she needed (not wanted) him. "She started whining, just like my wife. I ended the affair soon after that. I can get that kind of nagging at home."

The mistress mind-set offers empathy and understanding. It also calls for being able to put your needs temporarily aside. That is the enticement the mistress offers to many men. Just like your role as married mistress, using the appropriate mind-set is something you'll feel comfortable adjusting to when the situation calls for it. Knowing when takes a little practice, but in time, you'll realize when to react like a responsible mate and rationally question decisions that affect you, and when to react like the mistress or loving partner and become the most understanding arms he will ever desire.

Thirty

Use Your Love Kit

Love Tools

Your love kit holds the special tools to keep your intimate bond running in a loving direction. When you two became involved, it was brand new, and you kept it in mint condition. It contained all the tools you needed to propel your relationship to where it is today. It is full of:

- ♥ Love
- ♥ Commitment
- ♥ Lust
- ♥ Consideration
- ♥ Kindness
- ♥ Fantasies
- ♥ Fond memories
- ♥ Thoughtfulness
- ♥ Forgiveness
- ♥ Respect
- ♥ Positive thoughts

and many more wonderful emotions. But sometimes, after marriage, many wives' love kits get shoved under the bed. Some tools get lost. They forget that they have them and fail to keep them in working order.

Her Most Potent Secret:

> She has the same tools you do, but she *makes sure she keeps them in working order.*

A revelation for me when I interviewed women who had slept with married men was that they fully understand that they have nothing special or better than the wife has. When asked, "What do you have that she doesn't?" almost everyone of them answered a resounding, "Nothing." One woman in particular took this thought a step further. "I don't have anything his wife doesn't have," she staunchly admitted. *"She just doesn't use it."*

Her answer danced around in my head all night long. She was so imperious and self-assured when she told me that, but I had to admit, she was also right. Relationships cannot go stale unless the people involved allow them to. That's what happens when you or your mate stop using your love kits.

It's still there. The tools may be a little rusty from non-use, but you can clean them and use them again and again. You and the other woman have the same tools to work with. She's going to make certain that hers are always in working order. And she'll go one better. She'll put money on the fact that, as the wife, you will eventually shove your love kit under your bed and forget to use it until it's too late. That will give her the excuse to make her move.

So get it out. Polish those tools and keep them in working order. You can't indulge in a loving marital affair unless you employ every tool you have. By using your love kit, the next time the other woman accuses the wife of being neglectful, you'll be one less wife to live up to her expectations.

Thirty-One

Putting It All Together

Well, there you have it--the answers to the real lure of the other woman and to infidelity-proofing your marriage. You also have in your possession the key to enjoying an enriching marital affair with your mate. You understand how easy it is to play the role of the enticing married mistress. By adding this racy element to your relationship and indulging in a marital affair, your relationship will enjoy newfound excitement and revitalization.

Remember her secrets. Remember why men are so attracted to her. But most of all remember, *she doesn't have anything you don't*. As a married mistress, you hold the same lures she does, but none of the risk. Start your affair now. Remember, the definition of a married mistress is a woman who uses the power she possesses to make her intimate relationship, exciting, fulfilling, and monogamous. Together, you and your mate have the power to make your intimate relationship the best it can be.

Your Dream House

Marriage is like a dream house. When you purchase the house of your dreams you can't believe your fantasy materialized. You're on a euphoric high. Your dream house will always be fresh to you. But after walking through the same door year after year, your domestic coup becomes commonplace. You slowly come down off your electric high. After awhile, you even get a little bored with your familiar surroundings. That's when you begin to re-arrange the furniture, splash a new coat of paint on the grubby walls, and start storing "old things" in the attic.

One day, while visiting the attic to put away more "things" you've accumulated, you spot that dusty, emerald, boudoir lamp out the corner of your eye. You remember it was the first lamp your husband bought you to put on your nightstand so you could read your Danielle Steele novels until the wee hours of the night. As you dust it off, you begin to remember how you used to wake him up after reading the steamy parts so you could re-create the scene in his arms.

Then you spot that old faded teddy bear with one arm missing and fur patches eaten away by time. That bear takes you back into the delivery room when you held your newborn daughter for the first time, and your husband's eyes were shining with tears. You suddenly realize that this house may be familiar and it may be the same door you walk through day after day, but you know you wouldn't trade it for the million dollar mansion on the hill. It holds too many memories too dear. It will always be your dream house. You realize that you'll continue re-arranging furniture and painting the house to make the old seem new again--but it will always be home.

Marriage is no different. The electrifying high will fade with time, and every now and again you'll have to do some re-arranging in your lifestyle to make your seasoned relationship exciting. Use the marital affair to put a fresh coat of paint on your relationship. And keep all the fond, lasting memories you build together in your heart's attic.

If you see any weak links in your marriage, fix them. Take pains to make sure your marital fence is standing tall and strong. Remember, as a married mistress, you make sure your intimate relationship is exciting and fulfilling. Also make sure you take care of yourself and your needs.

This Is the Beginning

When you close the pages of this book, don't stop there. Let it be a beginning for you. Vow to work on making your relationship the best it can be. Don't let thoughts of your marital affair end here. Let it begin and flourish from here and make it better and better each day. Be sure to embroider your marital affair throughout your marriage and use the special threads of your embroidery to keep your intimate relationship alive with sensuality.

Take on your role as married mistress with enthusiasm. As the "mistress" in your man's life, you're red-hot and ready to enjoy a relationship brimming with fiery passion. Remember, when you indulge in an exciting marital affair with your love partner, you become the *only "mistress" your man will ever need.*

Bibliography and Recommended Reading

Adler, Mortimer J. *How to Speak/How to Listen.* New York: Macmillan, 1985.

Bailey, Covert. *Fit or Fat.* Boston: Houghton Mifflin, 1991.

Barry, Dave. *Dave Barry's Guide to Marriage, and/or Sex.* Pennsylvania: Rodale, 1987.

Berkowitz, Bob. *What Men Won't Tell You But Women Need to Know.* New York: Avon, 1990.

Blumstein, Philip, and Swartz, Pepper. *American Couples.* New York: Morrow, 1983.

Botwin, Carol. *Men Who Can't Be Faithful.* New York: Warner, 1988.

Bowder, Sue. "Let It Go." *New Woman,* October 1991, 94-96,98.

Bower, Sharon Anthony, and Bower, Gordon, H., *Asserting Yourself,* New York: Addison-Wesly, 1976.

Bright, Deborah. *Criticism in Your Life.* New York: Master Media, 1988.

Brothers, Joyce. *The Successful Woman.* New York: Simon and Schuster, 1988.

Brown, W. George, and Harris, Tirril. *Social Origins of Depression: A Study of Psychiatric Disorders in Women.* New York: Free Press, 1978.

Brown, Helen Gurley. *Having It All.* New York: Simon and Schuster, 1982.

Casey, Kathyrn. "Husbands Are Lousy Lovers." *Ladies Home Journal,* March, 1991, 68, 73-75.

Chesanow, Neil. "The Don Juan Syndrome." *Redbook,* April 1992, 98-101,118.

Cohen, Sidney, Ph.D., and Schwager, Michael. "A Common Language." *New Woman,* February 1991, 73-74.

Comfort, Alex. *The Joy of Sex.* New York: Crown, 1991.

Crenshaw, Theresa Larsen. *Bedside Manners.* New York: McGraw Hill, 1983.

De Angelis, Barbara, Ph.D. *How to Make Love All the Time.* New York: Macmillan, 1982.

_____. "Why Black Lace Turns Him On." *Family Circle,* February 1992, 44-47.

Dormen, Leslie. "Honey You're a Great Lover...Not!" *Ladies Home Journal*, July 1992, 70,72,74-75.

Dyer, Wayne W. *Your Erroneous Zones,* New York: Funk and Wagnalls, 1976.

_____. *Pulling Your Own Strings.* New York: Funk and Wagnalls, 1978.

"The Dynamics, Implications and Treatment of Extramarital Sexual Relations for the Family Therapist." *Journal of Marriage and Family Therapy* 7 (October 1981): 489-495.

Edwards, John N., and Booth, Alan. "Sexual Behavior In and Out of Marriage: An Assessment of the Correlates." *Journal of Marriage and the Family* 38 (February 1976): 73-81.

"Extramarital Involvement: Fact and Theory." *Journal of Sex Research* 9 (3) (August 1973): 210-224.

Fields, Doug. *Creative Romance.* Oregon: Harvest House, 1991.

Fleming, Jo. *His Affair.* Pennsylvania: M. Evans, 1976.

Freudenberger, Herbert J., and North, Gail, *Women's Burnout,* New York: Doubleday, 1985.

Gold, Steven R., Ph.D., and Chick, David, M.A. "Sexual Fantasy Patterns as Related to Sexual Attitude, Experience, Guilt and Sex." *Journal of Sex Education and Therapy* 14 (Spring/Summer 1988): 18-23.

Goldberg, Herb, Ph.D. *The Hazards of Being Male.* New York: Signet, 1976.

Goldstine, Daniel, et. al. *The Dance-Away Lover.* New York: Ballantine Books, 1977.

Hadju, David. "How to Prevent Divorce." *Cosmopolitan*, April 1992, 252-255.

Harris, Marlys. "Five Words That Will Make You Happier." *McCall's*, March 1992, 68-77.

"Healthy and Disturbed Reasons for Extramarital Relations." *The Journal of Human Relations* 7 (4) (November 1971): 274-281.

Heath, Desmond, "An Investigation Into the Origin of Copious Vaginal Discharge." *Journal of Sex Research* 20 (May 1984): 194-209.

Helmering, Doris Wild, *Happily Ever After,* New York: Warner, 1986.

Hite, Shere. *The Hite Report on Male Sexuality.* New York: Alfred A. Knopf, 1981.

Hogan, Mary. "Secrets of a Long Lasting Marriage." *Woman's World,* September 17, 1991, 50-51.

J. *The Sensuous Woman.* New York: Dell Publishing, 1969.

Johnson, Sharon. "Too Close for Comfort?" *Family Circle*, September 25, 1990, 30-34.

Kelly, Sean. "The Secret Life of Men." *Harper's Bazaar,* February, 1988, 193,213-215.

Kinder, Melvyn, and Cowan, Connell. *Husbands and Wives. New York:* C.N. Potter, 1989.

Kinsey, Alfred C., and Pomeroy, Wardell B., and Martin, Clyde E. *Sexual Behavior In The Human Male.* Philadelphia and London: W.B. Saunders, 1948.

Kramer, Johnathan, and Dunaway, Diane. *Why Men Don't Get Enough Sex and Women Don't Get Enough Love.* New York: Pocket-Star, 1991.

Kriegel, Leonard. *On Men and Manhood.* New York: Hawthorn, 1979.

Kuriansky, Judith. *Sex...* New York: G.P. Putnam's Sons, 1984.

Landers, Ann. *The Ann Landers Encyclopedia A to Z.* New York: Doubleday, 1978.

Lanoil Witkin, Georgia, Ph.D. *The Female Stress Syndrome.* New York: New Market Press, 1984.

Lasch, Christopher. *The Culture of Narcissism.* New York: W. W. Norton, 1978.

Loren, Richard E.A., and Weeks, Gerald R., Ph.D. "Sexual Fantasies of Undergraduates and Their Perceptions of the Sexual Fantasies of the Opposite Sex." *Journal of Sex Education and Therapy* 12 (Spring/Summer 1986): 31-36.

Lorr, Maurice and Wunderlich, Richard. "Self-esteem and Negative Affect," *Journal of Clinical Psychology* 44 (1) (January 1988): 37-39.

"Marital Separation and Extramarital Behavior." *Journal of Sex Research* 19 (1) (Feb. 1983) 23-48.

Masters, William H., and Johnson, Virginia E., and Kolodny, Robert C. *Masters and Johnson on Sex and Human Loving.* Boston-Toronto: Little, Brown, 1986.

_____. *The Pleasure Bond. Boston-Toronto:* Little, Brown, 1975.

Meeker, Barbara Foley. "Equality and Differentiation of Time Spent in Paid Work in Two Income Families." *Sex Roles* 9 (10) (October 1983) 1023-1033.

McCarthy, Laura Flynn. "Stress Busters That Work." *Woman's Day,* April 21, 1992, 40,42,56.

McGill, Michael. *The McGill Report on Male Intimacy. New York:* Holt, Rinehart, and Winston, 1985.

Mithers, Carol Lynn. "Five Reasons Why Husbands Stray." *Ladies Home Journal,* September 1988, 124, 126, 183-184.

Murray, Linda. "Sexual Ecstasy." *New Woman,* April, 1992, 57-59.

Naifeh, Steven, and Smith, Gregory White. *Why Can't Men Open Up?* New York: Warner, 1984.

Patterson, Chandra, and Sullivan, Juanita. "Would You Love A Married Man?" *Essence,* September,1989, 82-84,128,130.

Peck, M. Scott, M.D. *The Road Less Traveled.* New York: Simon and Schuster, 1978.

Pearsall, Paul. *Super Marital Sex.* New York: Doubleday, 1987.

Phelps, Stanlee, and Austin, Nancy. *The Assertive Woman.* California: Impact Publishers, 1983.

Probert, Christina. *Lingerie in Vogue Since 1910.* New York: Abbeville Press, 1981.

Richardson, Laurel. *The New Other Woman.* New York: The Free Press, 1985.

Rhodes, Sonya. "Good Husbands Do Stray." *McCall's,* April 1992, 64, 72-75.

_____. "The Biggest Mistake Loving Wives Make." *McCalls,* May 1992 56,58-59.

Rohlfing, Carla, and De Browner, Diane. "Are You a Victim of Silent Stress?" *Family Circle*, September 3, 1991, 40,42-44.

Rubin, Theodore Isaac, M.D. *One to One.* New York: The Viking Press, 1983.

Seligman, Martin, Ph.D. "Be an Optimist in Two Weeks." *Self,* June 1992, 115.

Shaffer, Martin, Ph.D. *Life After Stress,* New York: Plenum Press, 1982.

Sills, Judith, Ph.D. "Getting Your Own Way." *Cosmopolitan,* April 1992, 218-220.

_____. "When You Hate the One You Love." *New Woman.* April 1992, 81-84.

Sobel, Dava, and Singer, Helen Kaplan M.D., Ph.D. "When Sex Hurts." *Redbook,* October 1991, 50,52.

Stern, Ellen Sue. "Too Many Expectations?" *New Woman,* October 1991, 42-44.

Travis, Robert P., Ph.D., and Patricia, Travis, M.A. "Intimacy Based Sex Therapy," *Journal of Sex Research* 12 (Spring/Summer 1986): 21-27.

Volk, Patricia. "Men vs Women." *Family Circle,* April 1992, 73-75.

Vollmer, Ryan. "Silent Partner." *Ladies' Home Journal,* April 1992, 64,66-71.

Waterman, Caroline K., and Chiauzzi, Emil J. "The Role of Orgasm in Male and Female Sexual Enjoyment." *The Journal of Sex Research,* 18 (2) (May 1982): 146-159.

Winoker, Scott. "What Happy Couples Do Right." *Redbook,* June 1991, 65-68,118.

Westheimer, Ruth. *Dr. Ruth's Guide for Married Lovers.* New York: Warner, 1986.

_____. *Dr. Ruth's Guide to Good Sex.* Massachusetts: G.K. Hall, 1983.

Zick, Cathleen D., and Smith, Ken R. "Marital Transitions, Poverty, and Gender Differences in Morality." *Journal of Marriage and the Family* 53 (May 1991): 327-336.

INDEX

About the Author

Rose Smith is enjoying a lustful love affair with her loving husband of over seven years. They live in Albuquerque, New Mexico with their two children. She is founder of the Married Mistress and Monogamous Male Seminars which teach couples the art of loving. She has been teaching self-improvement classes to women and men for over ten years and holds a Bachelor of Science in mass communication.

A Letter to You

I'd like to hear how having a marital affair has helped your relationship. Also, if you have any suggestions to add to the "75 Ways to Spice Up Your Love Life" or you have any love recipes you'd like to share please write to me in care of the publisher:

William Havens Publishing
PO Box 81064
Albuquerque, NM 87198-1064

Order Form

Start Your Marital Affair On A Telling Note!!

Order YOUR Married Mistress T-Shirt TODAY!

T-Shirt Reads: *I'm having an affair...with my husband*
OR   *I'm having an affair...with my boyfriend*

Colors available: black shirt with blue lettering
white shirt with blue lettering

☐ *"Husband" T-Shirt $19.95 Color (Circle one) Black--White*
Size (Circle one) Small--Medium--Large--Ext. Large

☐ *"Boyfriend" T-Shirt $19.95 Color (Circle one) Black--White*
Size (Circle one) Small--Medium--Large--Ext. Large

☏ **Telephone Orders:** Call (505)260-0369.   Have Your Visa or Mastercard ready.

✉ Postal Orders: William Havens Publishing
Married Mistress Dept.
P.O. Box 81064-S1
Albuquerque, NM 87198-1064 (USA)

NAME: _____

ADDRESS: _____

CITY: _____ STATE: _____ ZIP: _____

Sales Tax: Please add 5.9% for shirts shipped to New Mexico addresses

Shipping: Regular Postage & Handling $4.00 for the first shirt.
Add 50 cents for each additional shirt (allow three to four weeks for delivery)
Air Mail: $6.50 per package

Payment: ☐Check ☐Credit Card ☐Visa ☐Mastercard

Card number:_____ Exp. date: ____

Name on card:_____

Please make check payable to William Havens Publishing.